past and present

BRAZIL

Text
Beppe Ceccato

Art Director
Patrizia Balocco

Editing Supervision by
Valeria Manferto De Fabianis
Laura Accomazzo

Graphic Supervision by
Anna Galliani

Translation by
Barbara Fisher
A.B.A.

CONTENTS

1 The statue of Christ the Redeemer was inaugurated in 1931; it is the work of the French sculptor Paul Landowsky and stands 100 feet high on Corcovado, the hunchback mountain in Rio de Janeiro.

2-7 The elaborate map illustrated here shows Brazil in 1642 when the Dutch wanted to increase their power on the north-east coast.

3/6 Pao de Açúcar is a granite peak situated at the entrance to the Baía de Guanabara on the southwestern coast where Rio de Janeiro lies. There is an unusual story attached to its name: the Indians had called it Pau-nd-Acuqua, *solitary peak, but to the ears of the Portuguese it sounded like Pao de Açúcar, sugar loaf, and its distinctive cone shape resembled the clay moulds they used to make sugar loaves.*

This edition published in 1997 by TIGER BOOKS INTERNATIONAL PLC, 26a York Street Twickenham TW1 3LJ, England.

First published by Edizioni White Star. Title of the original edition: Brazil. © World copyright 1997 by Edizioni White Star, Via Candido Sassone 22/24, 13100 Vercelli, Italy.

ISBN 1-85501-938-8

Printed in Italy by Grafedit, (Italy). Colour separations by Magenta Lithographic Con., Singapore and Fotomec (Italy).

*To Sonia who helped me to see, understand
and love this remarkable country*

TIGER BOOKS INTERNATIONAL

*A*na Maria da Conceição, 57, comes from Colônia de Leopoldina, a small town in Alagoas State in the north of Brazil. She's been living in São Paolo for 30 years, having journeyed to the city like thousands of other north-easterners in search of a job and a better life. Ana didn't find a job, just occasional work as a *faxineira* (charwoman). She didn't even find a better life; she's been living for 10 years in a sewer pipe with a diameter of just over one metre on Marginal Pinheiros, the orbital motorway which is one of the most polluted parts of São Paolo. Every time it rains, with the torrential cloudbursts of the tropics, she has to run out into the street to avoid being swept away by the force of the water.

Some 350 kilometres further west, in the town of Bauru, also in São Paolo State, Dr. Gastão, a friendly gentlemen in his fifties who collects statuettes of St. Francis, runs the *Centro de riabilitação das lesões labio palatais* (Labiopalatine Malformation Rehabilitation Centre), nicknamed the *Centrinho* (little centre) by the residents of Bauru. The *Centrinho*, which specialises in malformations such as the harelip and the cleft palate, is the leading hospital of its kind in South America. It conducts advanced studies, and doctors even come from the USA to learn about new developments in the subject. The most interesting feature of the hospital is that it is open to all, rich and poor alike, and treatment is free.

These are just two of the hundreds of everyday stories typical of the largest country in South America. Total indigence and sophisticated technology, a high illiteracy rate and top-level universities, avant-garde architecture and cardboard shanty towns – this mass of contradictions is Brazil in the Nineties.

After 13 years of military dictatorship the country plunged into an unprecedented recession, fell into the clutch-

8 top The Rio Tapajós is one of the principal tributaries of the Amazon river. The city of Santarém was founded in 1661 at the point where it flows into the Rio Amazonas (in this stretch called the Rio Solimoes). Twenty-five miles or so outside the city, again on the Tapajós, is Alter do Chao, a resort with white beaches and crystal-clear waters.

8 bottom The river Amazon can be navigated all over Brazil from Tabatinga, on the border with Peru and Colombia, to its outlet at the town of Belém.

9 The Foz do Iguaçú, the Great Waters in Tupi-Guaraní, is in the south of Brazil on the border with Paraguay and Argentina. With its 275 waterfalls plunging into a void 2 miles wide this is one of the natural wonders of Brazil. The most impressive sight is at the Garganta do Diablo, the Devil's Throat, where 14 waterfalls drop into a gorge 295 feet deep. The falls are in a national park that reaches over the frontier into Argentina.

10-11 Dancing is a moment of aggregation in the aldeias, the native villages. A man never usually dances with a woman and vice versa. Only in the upper Xingu do the women dance resting their hand on the shoulder of their partner.

*10 top left
The Indian tribal chiefs are distinguished by their refined feather head-dresses and large wooden inserts in their lips. The chiefs, or* cacique, *are chosen according to the customs of the different tribes. Among the Borôr Indians, for instance, leadership does not pass from father to son but by maternal descent, because the son belongs to the mother's family not that of the father. The life led by the* cacique *is similar to that of the other members of the tribe and they have no special privileges.*

10 top right A small Kayapó Indian is wearing a traditional costume. Her face is painted with a vegetable dye called urucu *obtained from the seeds of the arnotto (Bixa orellana) a characteristic tree of tropical America with leaves similar to those of the lime tree.*

es of unscrupulous presidents, and was put back on its feet by an economic plan that has reduced hyper-inflation and stabilised the currency but not the money in people's pockets. Despite all this, Brazil is still imagined by Europeans as the land of fun, the Carnival of Rio, football, and pretty mulatto girls who offer their sensual curves at cut price; the mecca of sex tourism (now facing strong competition from Cuba) and land of clichés. It's true that this is one aspect of Brazil. Sensuality and *joie de vivre* are typical of the Brazilians, with their mixture of races, cultures and religions. The country is full of contrasts, from the hyper-civilised south with Curitiba, the model town where bus stops are designed so that the handicapped can get on and off buses easily and there's no litter in the streets, not even a cigarette end, to the lively chaos of the north-east, with Salvador de Bahia, the first city founded by the Portuguese, which is the centre of Afro-Brazilian culture and the realm of *candomblé* and the Yoruba deities, and cities like the huge São Paolo and the classic Rio de Janeiro, with its gently smiling statue of Christ the Redeemer, arms permanently outstretched to bless Guanábara Bay.
These very different cities are situated in a country 28 times the size of Italy, a country as big as a continent, which is larger than Western Europe and shares the same principles in life. Its people have a mild, gentle,

humorous character, and are always ready to joke, even if they live in a wood and cardboard shack. Their origin no longer counts. Italians and Arabs, Japanese and Africans no longer exist – only Brazilians. "I get annoyed when people say I should cultivate my African roots", says Carlinhos Brown, a well-known musician from Bahia. "I'm not African; my culture is this one, a combination of several cultures. I'm a Brazilian." It's no accident that, apart from sporadic episodes, Brazil has not produced revolutionary movements like the Shining Path in Peru, the Montoneros in Argentina or the Sandinistas in Nicaragua. The amount that Brazilians are willing to put up with is proverbial, and verges on masochism.

12-13 Sao Joao del Rei is one of the best-conserved towns on the Minas Gerais colonial circuit. It is famous for the splendid church of Sao Francisco de Assís, *surrounded by towering* coqueros imperiais, *coconut palms more than 130 feet high, and as the* birthplace of Tancredo Neves, *one of the best-loved Brazilian politicians who died in mysterious circumstances.*

Newspapers in Europe, and especially in Italy, hardly ever talk about any of this; the only exception is represented by the Spanish and Portuguese press which, presumably as a result of post-Colonialist interest or guilt feelings, gives extensive coverage to the tropical Third World. It no longer makes the headlines when street children are brutally murdered by death squads; it's not even news that despite the interest of singers, politicians and scientists, Amazonia is inexorably heading towards destruction. None of these events seem to matter because they're just a routine part of everyday life – normal occurrences in a Third World country.

Habit is always a bad thing. It makes for forgetfulness, and even the most appalling events take on a semblance of normality. The country's economic recession, terrible poverty and social injustice no longer make the headlines. Even the country's next anniversary, in the year 2000, may well pass unnoticed. For Brazil, it means 500 years of history. After five centuries of life, the country is still young and brimming with natural resources, imagination and adaptability. The challenge facing its government is to give 180 million people (which is what the population will amount to at the beginning of the third millennium) the opportunity to go to school, learn the lessons of their country's short history, get a job, and believe in a slightly fairer Brazil. Impossible? Perhaps, but with the Brazilians, you never can tell...

13 top The Teatro Amazonas *opera house in Manaus was built in 1896 to a design by the Italian Doménico de Angelis at the very height of the rubber boom that brought riches to the city. At the time Manaus was one of the most important river ports in the world.*

13 bottom The church of Sao Francisco de Assís, in Salvador da Bahia, dates from the 18th century and was entirely built with stones brought from Portugal. The interior, a triumph of colonial baroque style, is filled with gold leaf-covered inlays. More than a hundred pounds of this precious metal was used to decorate the church.

Venezuela

Colombia

Guiana

Surinam

French
Guiana

Pernambuco coast

Ilha de
Marajó

Manaus   Santarém   Belem   São Luis

Amazon River

Fortaleza

Rio Xingu

Serra do Roncador

Rio Araguaia

Rio Tocantins

Recij

Palmares

Peru

Rio São Francisco

Salvador

Mato Grosso

Cuiabá

Brasilia

Baia de Todos
os Santos

Bolivia

Goiãnia

Porto
Seguro

The
Pantanal

Belo Horizonte

Aracruz

Paraguay

Rio Paraná

Ouro Preto

Rio Paraguay

Bauru

Rio de Janeiro

Chile

São Paulo

Atlantic
Ocean

Curitiba

Argentina

Rio Paraná

Lagoa
dos Patos

Uruguay

Lagoa
Mirim

The valley of Bocaina, in Saõ Paulo

16-17 The Matriz de Sao Antônio at Tiradentes is an exultation of stucco and gold. It is said to be second only to Sao Francisco de Assís in Salvador da Bahia for the quantity of gold (more than half a ton) used. Tiradentes is a pretty colonial town and takes its name from the dentist, Tiradentes, Joaquim José da Silva Xavier, head of the Inconfidência independence movement of 1789. Betrayed, he was captured and butchered by the Portuguese.

18-19 The rivers of the Amazon can be divided into three types: with white, brown or transparent waters. The first, like the Amazon river itself, are rich in sediments which make the water usually whitish-yellow; the second have acid water lacking in mineral nutrients and the third a reduced suspension content.

Fernando de Noronha Archipelago

Amazon River near Santarém

A stretch of fluvial plants in Pantanal

On 21st April 1500, young Pedro Alvares Cabral, commanding 13 ships which had set sail from the Rio Tejo, Lisbon, on 8th March the same year, cried out for joy; after leaving behind the African islands of Cape Verde, already ruled by the Lusitanian crown, he had sailed west and sighted land. According to his calculations, he had finally discovered a new route to the Indies. At least, so he believed. In fact, the navigator had sighted the beaches of Porto Seguro in what is now the State of Bahia, Brazil.

Genoese navigator Christopher Columbus had made the same mistake eight years earlier when, acting on behalf of the powerful Spanish crown, he had landed on American soil (in the West Indies), convinced that he had sailed the China Sea and reached India.

20 Pedro Alvares Cabral claims the newly-discovered land for the Portuguese crown, for King Dom Manuel. Some historians believe that the Brazilian coasts had already been visited by the Portuguese before 1500, the official year of discovery.

20-21 Cabral landed in Brazil, on the coast of what is now Porto Seguro on 22nd April 1500. Actually, the day before, 21st April, the Portuguese admiral and his fleet had already disembarked close to Porto Seguro. The painting, kept in the National History Museum in Rio de Janeiro, is by Oscár Pereira da Silva (1867/1939).

A SEGVNDA ARMA DA DE PEDRAL | VARES CABRAL ANO DE 500

21 top The fleet of 13 ships with which Pedro Alvares Cabral sailed from the Rio Tejo, Lisbon on 9th March 1500, is shown here in a 1565 reproduction from Lisuarte de Abreu's book, kept in the Pierpont Morgan Library in New York.

22-23 The 1494
Treaty of Tordesillas
(Tordesilhas in
Portuguese) shown
here in a painting
by Antonio
Menendez and
conserved in the
Naval Museum in

Lisbon, fixed a new
demarcation limit
between the Spanish
and Portuguese
colonial empires
(approximately 600
kilometres west
of Cape Verde)
in favour of Portugal.

22 top Dom Joao II
(1455-1495) King of
Portugal commenced
and encouraged
Portuguese desires for
expansion. During his
reign the Azores,
Madeira, Cape Verde
and Sao Tomé were
discovered and
claimed, assuring
the ivory trade, slaves
and gold for his

country. Portugal
acted as an
intermediary
purchasing gold and
slaves from Guinea
and exchanging them
for European products
(Flanders, Germany,
Italy, England and
France); these were
then sold through
Flanders on the
European market.

23 top The Treaty of
Tordesillas modified
Pope Alexander VI's
(1431-1503) Inter
caetera bull of 1493
which divided the
world up in favour
of the Spanish crown.

The result of Columbus' discoveries
was the Treaty of Tordesillas, signed
on 7th June 1494 by His Majesty
João II of Portugal and the Catholic
King and Queen of Spain, Ferdinand
and Isabella. The treaty modified the
division of the world, pronounced the
previous year by Pope Alexander VI in
the Papal Bull *Inter caetera*, in favour
of Portugal. The Portuguese crown,
helped by the good advice of Duarte
Pacheco Pereira, a specialist in geography and cosmography who attended
the conference (and was also one of
the captains of Cabral's ships), was
authorised to take possession of all the
lands (and all the inhabitants) of the
New World which lay 600 kilometres
west of Cape Verde.

23 bottom
An excelente *was the*
Spanish gold coin in
circulation in the
16th century. The
opposite side shows the
sovereigns Ferdinand
of Aragon and
Isabella of Castile.
Christopher
Columbus discovered
America in 1492
during their reign.

24-25 Usually, in the native communities the men went hunting and defended the tribe, the women devoted themselves to agriculture and craftwork. The Europeans initially treated the Indians as an exotic whim, to be exhibited in the European courts, as in this representation of native life in Rouen, France, in 1550 in

honour of Henry II and Catherine de' Medici and shown in a print of the times.

24 top left In the chronicles of the times, provided by Jesuits and colonists, the good Indians were those who allied with the Portuguese, all the others who fought against them were bad. The Aimoré, for instance, who differed

from the other tribes for their military efficiency and rebel spirit, were always described by the chroniclers of the period (mostly Jesuits) as animals living in the forest: all the other Indians lived in houses. When the Crown published the first law banning Indian slavery (1570) only the Aimoré were specifically excluded.

24 top right At the time of colonization the Indians lived merely at survival level, procuring necessities for the consumption of the tribe. They felled trees and burnt the forest to cultivate wheat, beans,

marrows and manioc, a root which became the basic diet of Brazil. There were contacts between tribes who exchanged women and luxury goods, toucan feathers and the stones to make botoques, ornamental objects.

25 top Indian is an inappropriate name. Convinced he had discovered the Indies, Cabral baptized these Amerindian peoples Indians. It is hard to analyze the society and customs of the Indians because their entire history has been filtered by the Portuguese, who considered certain beliefs and habits to be truly barbarious.

Young Cabral, convinced that he had dropped anchor in the Indian Ocean, named the strange people who watched the large ships that had appeared out of nowhere "Indians". At that time, the population of Brazil was mainly concentrated in the coastal area of the country and the Rio Paraná-Paraguay basin (to the south).

This population was unrelated to the natives encountered by the Spaniards in central America and on the east coast of South America; the Maya were skilled observers of the stars, the Incas sophisticated jewellers and weavers, and the Aztecs had built an empire that impressed the conquistadors. The Brazilian Indians (divided into two main races, *tupí guaraní* and *tapuiá*) still lived in a semi-primitive state. They were sociable and simple; the women made pottery and farmed the land, planting beans, corn, pumpkins and above all cassava (cassava flour later became the staple food of the colony), while the men hunted, fished and defended the villages.

The arrival of the Portuguese was a catastrophe for the Indians. The discovery of Brazil can undoubtedly be described as one of the worst holocausts in history; the Indians were enslaved, exterminated by diseases unknown to them, forced to lead a

life of nothing but hard toil, and to give up their ancient customs. 500 years later, the tyranny still goes on. The church contributed to it with directives and local interventions, authorising and supporting the colonial policy of the two European super-powers; "the souls are God's and the land is the King's" was the Pope's motto.

25 bottom
The Indians who lived in Brazil when the Portuguese landed belonged to the Tupi-Guaraní stock.
The encounter with European culture for these peoples, who were not a nation proper but different tribes often at odds with each other, was devastating.

26 top left, right centre and bottom right and 27 top right The Botocudos Indians were thus called because they pierced the lobes of their ears, noses and chin to insert botoques. *Usually these were discs in worked stone inserted when they were children. The mouth inserts, now used by the* Cayapó, *deform the whole dental arch, curving it inwards.*

26 top right The Tupi-Guaraní Indians were nomads, frequently changing village according to the food and crops they managed to produce. With the arrival of the Portuguese the natives sought preservation through self exile, withdrawing to ever less explored and hospitable areas.

26 bottom left The objects used by the Brazilian Indians (seen here in a water-coloured lithography taken from the Galleria Universale di Tutti i Populi del Mondo, *Venice, 1841) were very simple but equally decorative.*

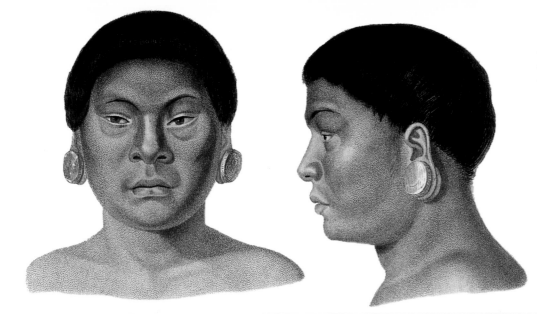

26-27 The Indians had a very strong sense of family but not in the common western sense of the word. The members of the same tribe usually lived in large huts, aldeias, *and shared everything.*

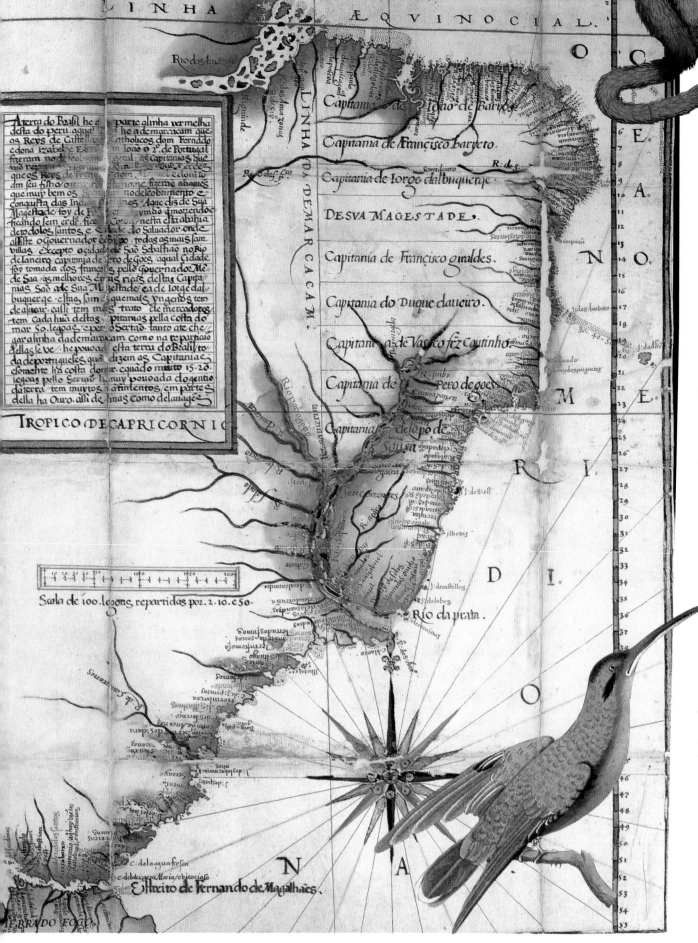

28 left The coast of
Brazil in 1579, 80
years after its
discovery, is shown
here in a print of the
period kept in the
Ajuda Library in
Lisbon.

LINHA   ÆOVINOCIAL.

Rio das Amazonas

Capitania de Ioão de Barros.

Capitania de Francisco barreto.

Capitania de Iorge dalbuquerqe.

DE SVA MAGESTADE.

Capitania de Francisco gualdes.

Capitania do Duque claueiro.

Capitania de Vasco frz Coutinho.

Capitania de   Pero de goes.

Capitania   delopo de
                   Sousa

TROPICO DE CAPRICORNIO

Scala de 100. legoas, repartidas por. 2. 10. e 50.

Rio da prata.

Estreito de Fernando de Magalhães.

28 top right and 29
top Monkeys, like the
tropical birds, struck
the imagination of
the colonists and were
used to adorn many
courts in Europe,
to the benefit of the
traders.

28 bottom right, 29
centre right and 29
bottom The tropical
birds greatly
fascinated the
colonists who started
a flourishing trade to
Europe. As well as the
araras, large parrots,
favourites were
toucans and
numerous species
of humming-birds.

29 centre left
A nautical chart
of circa 1540 shows
the Brazilian coasts.
After an initial
       period of
    adjustment,
trade with the mother
country became
increasingly intense.
The mercantilist
policy of Portugal
gave a sort of
monopoly to boats
flying the national
flag, the only ones
allowed to carry the
products of the colony
to Portugal. This was
done in an attempt to
stop foreign boats
transporting goods
produced in Brazil,
which could then be
sold directly in the
other European states
without Portuguese
involvement.

The new colony, which King Dom Manoel named Vera Cruz, and later Santa Cruz, did not arouse the same enthusiasm as Vasco da Gama's discovery of the sea route from Portugal to India three years earlier, in 1497. The Portuguese long believed that Brazil was merely a large island which offered nothing very interesting apart from Indians adorned with feathers, strange birds and macaws, the large colourful parrots. The fame of these birds was such that some Italian chroniclers of the peri-od described the country as "Parrot-land". The name Brazil began to be used in 1503, when it was realised that the wealth of the *Novo Mundo* lay in a tree called *pau brasil*; its red sap was used for dyeing, and its very strong wood to build ships and furniture. In the first 30 years after their discovery, the Portuguese did no more than explore the Brazilian coastline, collecting wood and exotic birds, without venturing into the interior. The first attempts to explore the coastal region were based on the

system of *feitorias*, fortified warehouses already used on the African coasts not only for the defence of the territory, but also for trade with the natives. Brazil was leased for three years to a consortium of traders from Lisbon, led by "new Christian" Fernão de Noronha. The consortium was granted the trading monopoly, and in exchange had to commission six ships a year to explore *trezentas léguas* (roughly 2,000 kilometres) of coast in the New World. The consortium did not live up to expectations, and on the expiry of the lease the crown commenced explorations alone.

30 top Martin Afonso de Sousa (seen here in a portrait of 1565) was sent by Dom Joao III to Brazil in 1530 with the task of reorganizing the new colony, patrolling the coastlines, extending Portuguese dominion and setting up hereditary captaincies. Martin Afonso's expedition marked a moment of transition from an initial period of adjustment to the desire to organize systematically the new land.

30 bottom Dom Joao III (1502-1557) was King of Portugal from 1521 until his death. Famous for having introduced the Inquisition into his country, in 1540 he divided Brazil up into captaincies and instituted a general government.

30-31 Once they had discovered the new land, the Portuguese had to defend it against attacks by other expanding colonial countries such as France, which with an expedition led by Nicolas Durand de Villegaignon attempted between 1555 and 1567 to found "Antarctic France" in the Baía de Guanabara, Rio de Janeiro.

It was not until the Portuguese conquests were threatened by adventurers from other European countries (especially the French, who refused to recognise the Treaty of Tordesillas, founded some colonies and indulged in piracy) that the Lusitanian crown began a full-scale policy of colonisation. The first "colonist" was Martim Afonso de Sousa. He arrived in Brazil in 1530 with specific instructions: to expel the French and extend the Portuguese dominions by patrolling the coast. In the course of his duties, which he performed with great zeal and few scruples towards the local populations, he founded São Vicente, where the first sugar cane plantations were introduced and cattle rearing began. At about the same time, Dom João III, King of Portugal, decided to divide Brazil into 15 parts, obtained by drawing a series of lines parallel to the Equator from the coast to the Tordesillas meridian, and entrusted their management to 12 captains-in-chief from 1534 to 1536. The new governors of the colony came from a wide variety of social backgrounds; minor nobility (those of high lineage were engaged in the more profitable trade with the Indies), ordinary civil servants and traders, who had links of some kind with the crown and extensive powers in the economic, administrative and legal fields. The experiment soon proved to be a failure, with only two exceptions: the Capitania of São Vicente and that of Pernambuco.

The crown then tried a new strategy, and in 1549 Tomé de Sousa, the first Governor-General of Brazil, arrived in Bahia. The chronicles of the period recount that he made his entrance to Salvador with a retinue of 1,000. Among them, as well as a small army, there were Jesuits and the scum of the Lusitanian prisons. The task of the new Governor was to colonise the country, while the Jesuits (the most famous and implacable soldier-priests being Manuel da Nóbrega and José da Anchieta) were sent to "colonise souls", i.e. to convert the natives to Catholicism and turn them into "good Christians", devoted only to work (needless to say as slaves) and to the Holy Mother Church. Systematic colonisation of the land and the Indians then began. It was based on

33 left Diamonds and gold mines represented one of the major resources of the new colony. In the regions of Bahia, Goiás in Mato Grosso but especially in Minas Gerais the production of diamonds, emeralds, imperial topaz, aquamarine, amethysts and gold reached incredible levels. The discovery of these mines was a magic touch for the waning Portuguese funds. The gold rush caused the first great wave of migration to Brazil, bringing approximately 600,000 people in the first 60 years of the eighteenth century.

32 left In 1549 Tomé de Sousa arrived in Salvador, appointed first governor general of Brazil. He arrived in Bahia with a following of more than a thousand people, of which 400 were exiles. Also with him was the Jesuit Manuel da Nóbrega, accompanied by five brothers who wished to convert the Indians to Christianity and discipline the few priests in the colony. Father Manuel was a member of the conservative clergy and became famous for his definition of the Indians: "dogs who eat each other and kill, and pigs in their vices and relationships".

32 top right The name of Bahia de Todos os Santos was given by the Portuguese sailors commanded by Amerigo Vespucci who discovered this bay on 1 November 1502. The city of Salvador da Bahia de Todos os Santos (the full name) was built in 1549 under Tomé de Sousa. The baroque monuments date from 1600 when the city became rich thanks to the diamond mines discovered in the Chapada Diamantina, splendid canyons approximately 370 miles into the state of Bahia.

32 bottom right Rio de Janeiro was founded on 1 January 1502 by André Gonçalves, a member of Amerigo Vespucci's Portuguese fleet. It was given this name because, to the eyes of the sailors, the huge Baía de Guanabara looked like the mouth of a great river, the river of January. The Tamois Indians who lived along that stretch of coastline called the newly-arrived Cariocas (white houses) as once settled on land, the Portuguese started to build brick houses that they painted white.

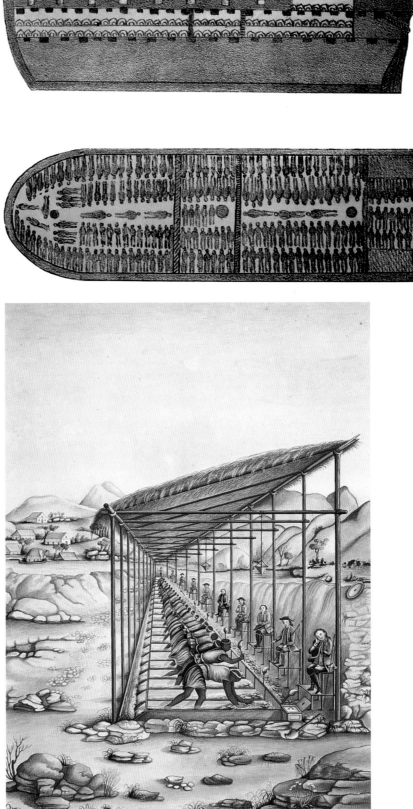

33 top right
The slave trade with slave ships was extremely profitable; it has been calculated that between 1550 and 1885 more than 4,000,000 slaves entered the ports of Brazil, most of them young men.

33 bottom right
Feitores, *armed with whips, kept a close watch over the slaves who used to wash the precious stones in the mines, as shown in this 18th-century watercolour conserved in the National Library of Rio de Janeiro.*

extensive agriculture, immigration by Portuguese colonists, the underprivileged and convicts, and unrestricted use of slaves – first Indians (who cost a third of the price of African slaves), and then Africans, bought or captured on the coasts of Guinea, the Congo and Angola, who were stronger and more productive than the Brazilian natives. At the same time the new order introduced into the colony began to take shape, and the population was divided into "pure" and "impure". The former were Portuguese citizens who were entitled to hold government office, receive titles, etc. The latter were all the others, called "new Christians": negroes, even if freed, Indians, and numerous types of half-castes. This distinction was abolished (though only on paper) by an Act passed in 1773.

The French and Spanish continued their raids until the early 17th century; the French founded Francia Antártica at Guanabara (Rio de Janeiro) between 1555 and 1567, and occupied the State of Maranhão, in the north-east of the country, between 1612 and 1615. Towards the end of the 16th century the Dutch arrived on the Brazilian coasts too. They had major interests in the new country; they controlled 60% of the maritime trade in sugar between Portugal and Brazil, and 25 refineries in Amsterdam refined sugar imported from Brazil. In 1624 the Dutch attacked Salvador, the headquarters of the central government (only to capitulate the following year), and held a coastal strip in the north-east for 24 years. This series of occupations gave rise to another great historical event, the creation of the *quilombo*s. These were fortified villages inhabited by African slaves who had escaped from

34 This map by Bleau, unique in its genre, shows the capitanias of Paraíba and Rio Grande. The drawings on top left and right show the conditions of local life at that time: a procession of Indians and a house perhaps near Pernambuco.

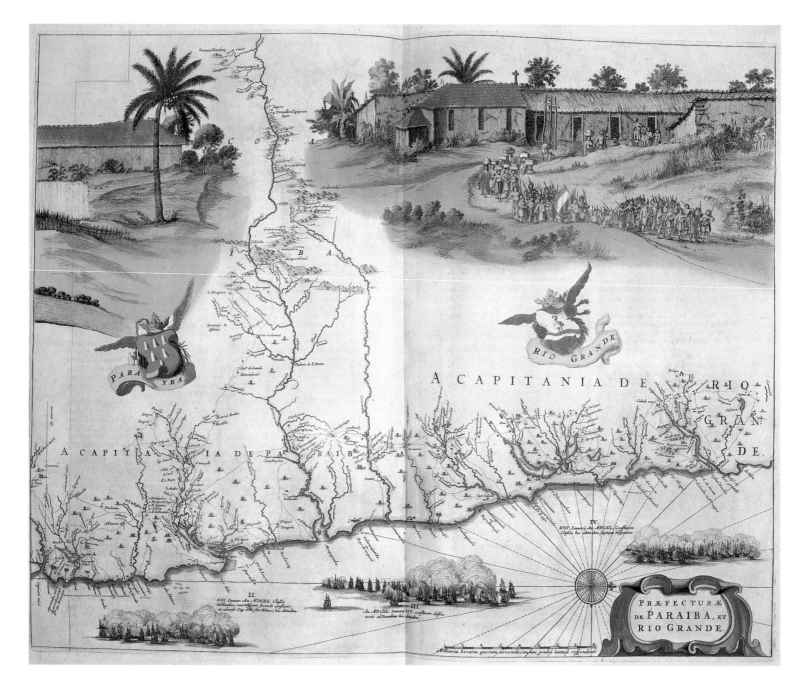

the plantations, the most famous being Palmares.

While Spain, France and Holland refused to recognise the Treaty of Tordesillas, the Portuguese Brazilians acted no better; they organised numerous expeditions into the interior of the country, beyond the famous 370 league strip. These raids were called *entradas* or *bandeiras*. The former were official explorations ordered by the crown, designed to consolidate Portuguese rule and fight the native rebels. The latter type of expedition was privately organised, mainly by inhabitants of São Paolo, to catch natives for use as slaves and to prospect for gem deposits. The most famous of all the *bandeirantes*, Antônio Raposo Tavares, travelled 12,000 kilometres; he set off from São Paolo and reached Mato Grosso do Sul, Mato Grosso, Rondônia and Pará.

35 right This map of Brazil by Joan Bleau draws its inspiration from a map bought by Willem Blaeu in 1629. Much more elaborated, it illustrates Brazil in 1642, when the Dutch were trying to colonize a part of the oriental coast of this big country.

35 top left From the time of its discovery, Rio de Janeiro has been known for its mountains and above all for Pao de Açúcar, sugar loaf, still Brazil's best-known view.

35 bottom left Pernambuco is shown in an early 17th-century atlas by W. Blaeu. It is thanks to the Prince of Nassau that Recife, the capital, and nearby Olinda, were embellished with splendid baroque monuments.

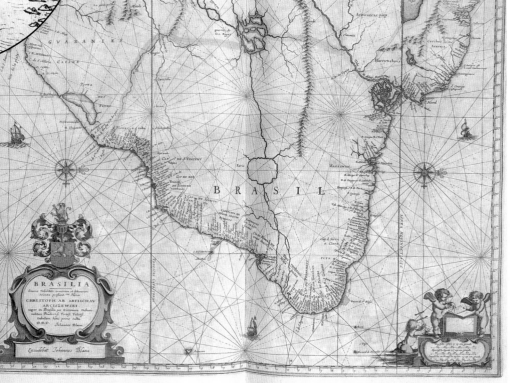

36-37 With the 1826
treaty, Britain had to
inspect the Brazilian
ships. This led to the
sequestration of many
slave-ships. In 1850
the Brazilian
parliament passed
a law outlawing
the slave trade. The
number of Africans
entering the South
American country fell
from 23,000 in 1850
to 3,300 just a year
later.

At the beginning of the 18th century, Portugal lost its role as a European super-power. This was demonstrated by the signature in 1711 of the Treaty of Methuen with England, which placed the Lusitanians in a position of economic dependence and allowed the entry of English textiles to their territory. At the same time Brazil was growing increasingly aware of being a state until itself, separated from Portugal not only by the Atlantic Ocean, but also by very different customs and lifestyles. In the second half of the 18th century the battle for independence by the British colonies in North America (1776) and the French Revolution (1789), together with the beginnings of the English industrial revolution in Europe, galvanised the attention of the new Latin population, especially the inhabitants of São Paolo and Minas Gerais, the two wealthiest and most culturally dynamic states. Independence movements flourished, such as *Inconfidência Mineira* (which demanded a republic on the lines of the American republic), led by dentist José Joaquim da Silva Xavier, known as Tiradentes (tooth-puller). Tiradentes was eventually betrayed, tried and condemned in a long judgment (which took the judges 18 hours to read), then hung, drawn and quartered. His head was taken to Ouro Preto, then the capital of Minas, and displayed in the main square. Another revolt was that of the artisans, mainly mulattos and freed black slaves, called the *revolta dos Alfaiates* (the tailors' revolt) because tailors joined the movement en masse; the rebels demanded a republic, an end to slavery, free trade (especially with France) and an increase in soldiers' pay. This rebellion was also firmly put down.

Then, in 1807, something happened which changed Brazil's destiny; ousted by the unstoppable advance of Napoleon's army, the Portuguese court hastily moved to Brazil. Between 25th and 27th November that year, 15,000 people embarked for the colony under the protection of the English army.

The Portuguese King Dom João VI rewarded the English for their help by opening the Brazilian ports to his European friends. The court settled in Rio de Janeiro. Dom João conquered Uruguay, and in 1808 the first printed newspaper was published in Brazil, and the Kingdom's first bank, Banco do Brasil, was opened. Rio became a major cultural centre, with theatres, libraries, and literary and scientific academies. During the period of the King's residence, the population of the capital doubled, from 50,000 to 100,000. Many of the new residents were Portuguese, Spanish, French and English immigrants, who formed a middle class of small businessmen and skilled craftsmen.

38 bottom right The embarkation of the Brazilian troops at Praia Grande for the war against Uruguay in 1816. On that occasion the Brazilians allied with Argentina and the expedition was authorized by Dom Joao VI.

38 left Dom Joao VI (1767-1826) was appointed prince regent of Portugal in 1792, when his mother Dona Maria I was declared mad. He allied with Britain during the Napoleonic wars and, when the French troops invaded Portugal in 1807, he took refuge with his entire court of

scientists, artists and intellectuals in Brazil. He was declared King in 1816 on his mother's death (the ceremony was celebrated in Rio de Janeiro).

38 top right This gold coin dating from the reign of John V of Braganza, King of Portugal, was

commonly used in the viceroyalty of Brazil from 1714. The gold to make the coin came from the gold mines of the southern regions.

38 centre right This 1839 engraving by J. B. Debret shows the acclamation of king Dom Joao VI in Rio de Janeiro.

The Portuguese revolution of 1820 and the consequent repercussions in Brazil persuaded Dom João to embark for Europe in April 1821, accompanied by 4,000 Portuguese. His son Pedro stayed in Brazil. In the meantime, the pressure for independence from a pro-Brazil faction became increasingly strong, and on 9th January 1822 Prince Dom Pedro announced his decision to remain in Rio in the famous speech which began "Tell the people I'm here to stay". That day was known to Brazilians ever after as *o dia do fico* ("I'm here to stay day"). The country had burned its boats, finally severing its links with Portugal.

On 7th September the same year, on the Ipiranga river, Dom Pedro declared the colony independent,

and at the age of only 24, he became Dom Pedro I, Emperor of Brazil. In 1824 the first constitution was introduced, guaranteeing a hereditary constitutional monarchy. Legislative power was divided between the Chamber of Deputies and the Senate, and the country was divided into provinces, whose presidents were appointed by the Emperor. In 1825 Portugal recognised the independence of Brazil, but as compensation for the loss of the colony claimed damages amounting to 2 million libras and an agreement not to persuade other Portuguese possessions to declare independence.

40 Dom Pedro II (1825-1891) was Emperor of Brazil from 1831, the year his father Pedro I fled to Portugal, until 1889, when Brazil was proclaimed a republic and Pedro II himself was exiled to France. Slavery was abolished during his reign.

41 top left Giuseppe Garibaldi (1807-1882) also fought in Brazil supporting the Farrapos rebellion in Rio Grande do Sul (1839-1841), thus called because, the farrapos, *or wretches, joined forces with the rich landowners. During those years Garibaldi met and married the Brazilian Anita.*

The reign of Dom Pedro, first Emperor of independent Brazil, lasted until 7th April 1831, when he was forced to abdicate in favour of his son, Dom Pedro II. Secessionist rebellions, a lost war with the United Provinces of Rio della Plata (the future Argentina) which emptied the coffers of the State, the continually falling prices of coffee, hides, cocoa, tobacco and sugar (at a time when the sugar market was already facing a crisis because of the entry onto world markets of Cuba, a major cane producer), the crisis of the Banco do Brasil and the minting of easily counterfeited copper coins, plunged Brazil into an economic depression, and the Emperor was

forced to abdicate. The accession of Dom Pedro II marked the beginning of the Regency period, one of the most tumultuous in the history of the young country; revolts in the north and north-east and the *revolta dos farrapos* (the beggars' revolt) in Rio Grande do Sul, in which Giuseppe Garibaldi took part (1835), characterised the years until 1840, when Dom Pedro II took possession of the throne, which he kept until 1889. During this period, slavery was banned (*Lei Àurea*, 1888) under pressure from the English, who had been calling for its abolition for years.

41 bottom left The photo shows the funeral of Dom Pedro II, who died in exile in France in 1891. Dom Pedro's reign passed without bloody revolts and made way for the new Republic.

41 right The Aurea law (the original text is conserved in the National History Museum in Rio de Janeiro) of 13 May 1888 officially abolished slavery in Brazil.

42 top left Cangueiros
Indians are carrying a
big and heavy barrel.
This is again a print
by Jean Debret.

42 bottom left
The sugar industry
was central to the
social and economic
life of the Brazilian
Northeast, Pernambuco
and Bahia.

42 top right In the ten
years between 1870
and 1880 coffee
represented 63% of
the total value of
Brazilian exports
climbing to 78% in
the Twenties.

42 centre right Coal
and of corn sellers are
shown here in an 1834
print conserved in the
National Library of
Rio de Janeiro.

The Brazilian economy was based on the cultivation of coffee (52.7% of exports), and rubber in the Amazon basin; between 1898 and 1910, rubber accounted for 25.7% of exports. 1891 was another crucial year; the new Republican constitution, based on the North American model, was passed, and the first waves of immigration from Europe began. The reign of Dom Pedro II ended without revolts or internal strife, making way for the republic.

Between 1887 and 1930 3,800,000 people entered Brazil. The period of greatest immigration was between 1887 and 1914, when 2,740,000 people landed (72% of the total).

The immigrants settled in the mid-south, and south-east of Brazil.

The State of São Paolo had the highest number of resident foreigners – 52.4%. Italians formed 35.5% of the immigrants in this major wave, followed by Portuguese (29%) and Spaniards (14.6).

The end of the monarchy also led to

the development of new power bases within the state; one of the strongest was the military, whose power reached its peak 80 years later with the 20-year-long dictatorship (1964-84). The military came from the lower middle classes, from the developing bourgeoisie which was soon to dominate the country, fomenting revolts and upholding their rights against the landowners' oligarchy.

42 bottom right Sugar
cane was one of the first
crops introduced to
Brazil. The Dutch
financed the production
of Brazilian sugar.

43 Gold mining
on Itacolomy, the
mountain shaped like
a curved Indian
woman, that
dominates Ouro Preto,
in the state of Minas
Gerais, made the
fortune of this city.

The central government was dominated by the two most economically powerful states, São Paolo and Minas Gerais. The First Republic was based on the convenient principle known as *café com leite*, whereby a President of the Republic from São Paolo alternated with one from Minas Gerais. The reins of power in Brazil were therefore held by gold and black gold – coffee. President Washington Luís broke with this tradition in 1929; he named as his successor Júlio Prestes from São Paolo,

who was elected in 1930. However, the nomination was not accepted by either Minas Gerais or Rio Grande do Sul, and on 3rd October 1930 the spark of revolution was lit, again with the support of the military. In a fortnight the army took control of the whole country, and appointed Getúlio Vargas provisional President of the new republic. The effect of the coup was to depose the old coffee barons, strengthen central power and allow the rise of reformist sectors of the lower-middle class from which Vargas himself hailed. Getulio Vargas is considered the most interesting politician in 20th-century Brazilian history. He came from south Brazil, of farming stock, and followed the classic political career, climbing all the rungs of the ladder to power. He remained at the helm of the country for 25 years. His policy was based on nationalism and populism; he was very popular with the Brazilians because for the first time he guaranteed a minimum wage, a

social security system, state schools, libraries, medical assistance and maternity leave. The trade unions were legalised, although they were responsible to the federal government. The Roman Catholic Church was a valuable ally to Vargas; from the time of the provisional government it guaranteed that the Catholic masses would support the State. In exchange, the government passed measures favourable to the Church, such as the teaching of religion in state schools. The union between temporal and spiritual dominion was symbolised by the statue of Christ erected in Rio de Janeiro. When it was inaugurated on 12th October 1931, Cardinal Leme consecrated the nation *"ao coração Santíssi-*

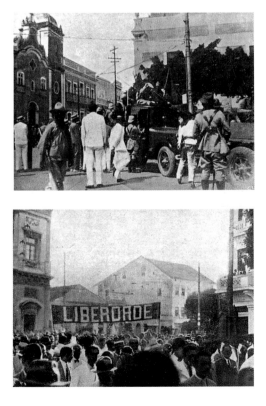

mo de Jesus, reconhecendo-o para sempre seu Rei e Senhor" (to the sacred heart of Jesus, acknowledging Him always as its Lord and King). The provisional government ended with a new Constitution in 1934, and Vargas was elected full President of Brazil. In 1937, with the excuse that there was an imminent risk of a Communist coup, Vargas, supported by the military, dissolved Congress (which continued to represent a classist group), abolished the constitutional charter, and drafted another in which he was given almost absolute powers. Brazil entered the era of the *Estado Novo* and the years of dictatorship, which resembled the Fascist rule of Benito Mussolini in many respects. Like Italy, Brazil also had its propaganda ministry, the famous *Departemento de Imprensa e Propaganda* (Press and Propaganda Department), which was directly responsible to the President of the Republic. Every day the Brazilians had to put up with the *Hora do Brasil* (Brazil Hour) on the radio, a programme that was later inherited by the military dictatorship, and still exists today, with democracy in full swing. Torture and exile were commonplace. As for foreign policy (these were the years of the Second World War), the *Estado Novo* originally tried to maintain a neutral stance in the conflict between the Allies and the Axis powers. Later, under pressure from the Americans, who had obtained air bases in the north and north-east of the country in 1942, and as a result of huge demonstrations which called for

Brazil to join the Allies, Vargas gave way, and 25,000 Brazilian soldiers were sent to fight with the American Fifth Army in Italy. 450 of them died, and are commemorated by a monument in Rio de Janeiro, on the Esplanada do Flamengo. With the Allied victory, the Fascist state headed by Vargas also came to the end of the line, and in 1945 Vargas was deposed by the same soldiers who had helped him in his rise to power 15 years earlier.

Vargas' fortunes began to wane. After a botched attempt by his followers to murder Maurício Lacerda, socialist leader of the opposition, the President, deciding that all was lost, shot himself in the heart. It was 24th August 1954.

On the death of Vargas, the last period of the Republic before the military dictatorship began. Juscelino Kubitschek from Minas Gerais was elected President. After encountering some difficulty in taking office (a military coup was required to instal him, despite the fact that he was duly elected by the people – a unique case in the history of coups d'état), he based his policy on the Programme of Goals. The Programme was designed

46 bottom right Maurício Lacerda is greeted joyously in Rio de Janeiro at the end of the October revolution. Repeatedly imprisoned for his socialist ideas, Lacerda was the first to appeal to the new Labour Law code in Parliament. At first in harmony with Getúlio Vargas, he then became a sworn enemy of the dictator, so much so that men loyal to the president tried to kill him in 1954.

46 left Eurico Gaspar Dutra (1885-1974) became general after bloodily repressing the Constitutionalist revolution of 1932 in Sao Paulo. He also led the battle against the communist rebellion of 1935. Minister of War from 1936 to 1945 under Vargas, he organized the military forces sent to Italy with the Americans during the Second World War.

46 top right Getúlio Vargas announces the members of the new cabinet in February 1951. Opposed by Congress and the political forces, the decline of the old dictator had begun and in 24 August 1954 he committed suicide, shooting himself in the heart.

After Vargas was ousted, Eurico Gaspar Dutra, War Minister under the dictator, was elected President. In 1946 another Constitution was passed; the country was defined as a Federal Republic, and the President of the Republic, elected directly by the people, was to hold office for 5 years. In the subtle world balance of the Cold War, Brazil, which now had very strong ties to the USA, acted as the South American bulwark against the threat represented by Communism and the populist trade unionism of Argentinian Juan Domingo Perón. The Communist Party was outlawed and US culture became increasingly dominant; the cinemas showed only Hollywood films, and the most popular magazine was *Reader's Digest Selection*, which defended the American way of life.

During the Dutra period, the indefatigable Getúlio Vargas prepared for his return, which was almost a foregone conclusion, on 31st January 1951. However, Congress and the opposition forces were hostile, and

Batista, who was supported by the Americans. Castro allied Cuba with the USSR, and the US deliberately fomented fear of the Communist threat, which spread all over Central and South America. Jânio liked Castro, however; he visited Cuba in 1960 and decorated another legend of the revolution, Ernesto Che Guevara, with the *Ordem do Cruzeiro do Sul* (Order of the Southern Cross), to the fury of the conservatives. Following accusations that he was planning a coup, he was forced to resign on 25th August 1961.

47 top Dwight David Eisenhower, President of the USA, visits Juscelino Kubitschek, President of Brazil, greeted in Rio by a cheering crowd in 1960.

47 bottom Jânio Quadros da Silva (1917-1992) was elected to the highest state office in October 1960 and lasted for one year.

to meet 31 targets divided into 6 major groups: energy, transport, food, basic industry, education, and the construction of Brasilia, commissioned from the brilliant Oscár Niemeyer and Lúcio Costa. Brasilia, called "the Goal that embraced all the others", was solemnly inaugurated on 21st April 1960. In October of the same year Jânio Quadros was elected President. He governed in an unorthodox fashion, dealing with matters which were not strictly speaking the President's province; for example, he banned the lança-perfume (a canister containing hallucinogenic substances used at carnival time), bikinis on the beaches and cock-fighting. In 1959 the delicate Latin American balance was upset by the victory of Fidel Castro and his *barbudos* over dictator Fulgencio

48 top left 1968 exploded in Brazil, which had for four years been under a fierce military dictatorship, but the student revolts were harshly repressed. The same year saw the birth of armed revolutionary groups against the government: Aliança de Libertaçao Nacional *of Carlos Marighella (killed by the military the following year), the* Movimento Revolucionário 8 de otubro *(MR-8) and* Vanguarda Popular Revolucionária *(VPR), the latter with a strong left-wing military component.*

The nomination of João Goulart, the Vice-President who should by rights have taken office on Quadros' resignation, was suspended by the military, who considered him too left-wing (Goulart happened to be making an official visit to China at the time). Some generals forbade his return to Brazil, while others supported him. The crisis almost led to civil war, but was ended by a compromise solution whereby Congress changed the system of government from presidential to parliamentary; Goulart remained in office, but subject to limitations.

48 right Artur da Costa e Silva (1902-1969), soldier and politician, was elected President of Brazil by the National Congress (1967-1969) but was removed from office before the end of his mandate following a stroke.

48 bottom left The student demonstrations continued, especially in Rio de Janeiro and São Paulo, and the police shot at body height killing demonstrators. The students met in front of the American consulate to protest; this was when the United States policy in Latin America became perverse. After Brazil came Chile and other Central American countries.

49 *Students,*
professors, artists and
priests, all filled the
streets to protest
against the regime
of Artur da Costa
e Silva, who left the
government the
following year.
In the meantime the
first bomb exploded
in front of the
American consulate
in Sao Paulo.

However, this situation didn't last long. In 1963 a national plebiscite called for the return of presidential government. Goulart regained full powers, promised social reforms, and threatened to nationalise foreign companies. Inflation, inherited from his predecessors, was sky-high, life was getting more expensive every day, and strikes and demonstrations were rife. On 31st March 1964, alleging that Goulart was planning a Communist coup, the military took over. Goulart fled to Uruguay, and for the fourth time since 1945, the army drastically interfered with the political life of Brazil. This last interference was to last the longest: for 21 years.

In 1968 General Arthur da Costa e Silva, successor of Castelo Branco, approved yet another new Constitution. Protests by the young, who had witnessed the radical changes in Europe and the USA, together with acts of armed resistance, made the regime clamp down on opposition. This was the most tragic period of Brazilian history – the years of torture, *desaparecidos* (missings) and exile. Congress was closed down, and the government could arrest anyone without giving any reason. In the meantime, almost paradoxically, the economy of the Latin American giant continued to grow, so much so that in the Seventies the economic boom was called *Milagre Brasileiro* (the Brazilian Miracle). The gross domestic product grew at an average rate of 11.2% per annum, and inflation stood at 18%.

The economic boom came to an end
in the Eighties. During the prosperity
of the previous decade deprivation of
freedom and civil rights had been
ignored, but when the recession
came, the people woke up. João
Figueredo, who had promised to
restore democracy, announced an
amnesty for political prisoners and
exiles; censorship was abolished, new
parties were founded, and elections
were held for governors and Congress. However, this more or less
complete return to freedom was
accompanied by a much worse recession, and the foreign debt reached
the highest levels of the century. In
January 1985 an electoral body
formed by members of Congress and
the government appointed Tancredo
Neves President, but he died not
long afterwards. No-one knows what

really happened to the democratic Tancredo, in whom the entire Brazilian population had placed their trust. After being taken suddenly ill, he underwent an emergency operation, strangely in the presence of politicians and friends. After another operation in São Paolo, Tancredo died on 21st April 1985, a symbolic date for the country, because it marks the anniversary of the death of Tiradentes, hero of the *Inconfidência*. At the Planalto (the Presidential Palace), Vice-President José Sarney took office. The recession absorbed the attention of the entire Sarney administration, which attempted to check inflation by introducing the *Plano Cruzado*; prices were frozen but wages were allowed to rise. The effect was a false boom which left the Brazilians with no savings, but Sarney was more popular then ever.

51 top left José Sarney was the first non-military president elected at the end of the dictatorship in 1985.

51 bottom left On 28 February 1986 President José Sarney announced the application of the Plano Cruzado. *The old currency, the* cruzeiro, *was replaced by a strong one, the* cruzado, *in the proportion of 1,000 cruzeiros for 1 cruzado. Indexation was abolished, prices and exchange rates frozen and the minimum salary was increased. The price freeze was greeted with demonstrations in support of the President and with reckless spending.*

51 right In November 1982, after exactly 17 years, more than 48,000,000 Brazilians voted to elect the town councils and state governors. The Partido Democrático Social *(PDS) bound to the military, had to relinquish crucial positions such as governorship of the states of São Paulo, Minas Gerais and Paraná.*

In 1988 a new Constitution was introduced, and the north-eastern politician who loved painting and literature remained in office until 1990, when the first democratic elections since the dictatorship were held. Brazil then went from the frying pan into the fire. By flaunting the most vulgar populism, a mysterious young politician from Alagoas, Fernando Collor de Mello (one of the 5% of the Brazilian population who own 95% of the country's wealth) managed to get

elected, beating Luís Inacío da Silva, known as Lula, a former trade unionist and leader of the PT (the Workers' Party). The election was not fought on serious political or economic issues, but on an exchange of accusations and smear campaigns, aided by the television networks.

It must be admitted that neither candidate was equal to governing a country like Brazil. However, Collor, supported by the powerful Roberto Marinho, owner of Rede Globo, the largest TV network in Brazil, managed to win over the poorest classes, and defeated his rival by just a few votes. In the meantime, inflation had risen to 1700% a year. The first act of the new President on taking office was to freeze all Brazilians' savings without notice, promising that this forced loan to the State would be repaid with interest in 18 months. Brazil plunged into a terrible recession; many small businessmen who suddenly found themselves with no money to pay wages or buy materials committed suicide, and the *favelas* grew to accommodate the new poor. Amid all this chaos it was discovered by two journalists (in an odd parallel of the Watergate scandal) that Collor was mixed up in some very shady dealings and above all, that he had embezzled as

much as possible from the already impecunious State of Brazil. His impeachment was inevitable, and huge demonstrations from Brasilia to São Paolo forced the arrogant young President to leave the Planalto. He was succeeded by Vice-President Itamar Franco, who remained in office until the end of 1994. The rest is present-day history; the voters have now elected Fernano Henrique Cardoso, 65, world-famous sociologist, professor at the Sorbonne and former Labour Minster under Itamar Franco. All the progressive politicians, including Lula, have been inspired by his books. He must take the credit for beating the runaway inflation; when he was Treasury Minister in the previous government he introduced the *Plano Real*, as a result of which inflation plummeted from 150% a month to 2%.

When talking about nature in Brazil, the Amazon basin immediately comes to mind. The great Amazon rain-forest attracts all the attention because it occupies over half the country, but Brazil is so huge that its biodiversity is endless. For example, of the 290,000 species of higher plants existing on earth, 90,000 grow in Latin America, most of them in Brazil. Scientists believe that one in ten of the 1,400,000 species of living creatures in the world are to be found in Brazil. To convert these astonishing percentages into figures, the largest country in South America is home to 3,000 species of land-dwelling vertebrates, 3,000 species of freshwater fish, 55,000 species of flowering plants, 575 species of amphibians and 61 species of primates, not to mention reptiles (467 classified species) and birds (1,622 species). Although many of these creatures live in the Amazon basin, the Pantanal, is not far behind. The Pantanal (which means swamp or marshland) is a basin dating from the Quaternary era, the remains of an inland sea that started to dry up 65 million years ago. The sea was surrounded by tall peaks: the Serra de Maracaju to the east, the Bolivian Chaco to the west and the Serra do Roncador to the north. It is situated right in the middle of South America, is as large as France (230,000 square kilometres), and is shared by two Brazilian states (Mato Grosso and Mato Grosso do Sul), Paraguay and

*54-55 During the
rainy season in the
Pantanal, from
October to March, the
level of the rivers rises
by as much as 10 feet.
They flood their banks
to form pools where fish
reproduce and patches
of dry land where
animals take refuge.
For the caimans this is
the best feeding season.
During the dry season
they eat only insects
and small amphibians.*

*54 top left
The Pantanal, a huge
wetland stretching for
88,000 square miles
across the Mato Grosso,
Mato Grosso do Sul,
Paraguay and Bolivia,
is home to 600
different bird species,
including the biguá
(Phalacrocorax
olivaceus).*

*54 top right An ema
(Rhea americana), or
emu, the American
ostrich, also lives in
Brazil. It grows to a
maximum height of 4
feet and feeds on fruit,
grain and small
animals. The male can
sit on up to 40 eggs laid
by different females.*

Bolivia. Brazil contains just over half of it. Water is ever-present in the Pantanal, with its small streams, rivers, ponds and lakes, all joined and intersecting in an intricate navigable network.

This *Terra de Ninguem* (No Man's Land), as it is aptly nick-named in these parts, is actually a paradise for birdwatchers and nature-lovers, who can observe 600 species of birds

56-57 One of the most interesting Bahian beaches is Praia do Forte, a fashionable seaside resort, with a station for the observation and care of the sea turtles that flock to this coastline to lay their eggs.

56 top Canoa Quebrada, 105 miles from Fortaleza, is a fishing village that has fortunately been well-preserved. In the Seventies it was popular among hippies who came here seeking nature, freedom and a simple lifestyle.

together with the ever-present jacaré (a type of alligator), crocodiles, iguanas, jaguars, deers, otters, giant and dwarf anteaters, monkeys and tapirs. The water that fills the pools of the Pantanal flows down from the surrounding mountains. The same mountains generate the River Paraguay which, channelled towards the south, flows into the Atlantic. The region can be visited only from April to September (visitors to Brazil can make their base in the town of Cuiabá, on the border between the Amazon basin and the Pantanal). The rest of the year, during the rainy season, it is practically flooded. The countryside changes: the streams turn into rivers and the dry land into islands called *cordilheiras*, where animals take refuge.

From the swamps to the forest; not the Amazon basin, but the Mata Atlântica, which stretches from the north-east to Paraná, a state in the south of Brazil. This was the huge ancient forest encountered by the Portuguese colonists when they disembarked for the first time. The Mata Atlântica, characterised by dense areas of forest containing a wealth of plant species, tall trees and a wide variety of fauna including parrots, toucans and seagulls, is seriously endangered by the large conurbations that have developed over the centuries (especially São Paolo), and by the planting of trees that have altered the bioclimate. One example is the cellulose factory at Ara Cruz, in the State of

Espírito Santo, where eucalyptus has been planted in huge quantities; this tree, used to make paper, absorbs so much water that other plants are deprived of nourishment.

One of the best-preserved sections of the Mata Atlântica (the other is to the south of São Paolo, in the Vale do Ribeira, with 35,000 square kilometres of forest protected by a National Park set up in 1958) is the

57 bottom The scenery of the litoral norte, between São Paulo and Rio de Janeiro is truly spectacular and especially so between Ubatuba and Parati, one of the best preserved historic cities in Brazil, dating from the 18th century.

58 top The Parque
Nacional Aparados
da Serra stands on
the boundary between
the Rio Grande do
Sul and Santa
Catarina. This wide
canyon, 150 miles
from one extreme to
the other, divides the
two Brazilian states.
Plunging 2,200 feet
in some parts it was
created some 200
millon years ago by
volcanic eruptions.

58 bottom Mata
Atlântica used to be
a vast rainforest
stretching from south
Brazil to the
Northeast. Little
remains of this huge
green space that was
once on a par with
the Amazon. Traces
of Mata Atlântica
are to be found in the
states of São Paulo
and Rio de Janeiro.

mountain chain called the Juréia (which in the Tupi-Guarani language means projecting tip), a huge massif that stretches down to the sea, on the São Paolo coast. It's a true paradise, with 40 kilometres of unspoilt beaches, over 400 species of medicinal plants and hundreds of species of animals, especially birds; yet it's only 200 kilometres from the chaotic São Paolo and 130 kilometres from Cubatão, a town sadly famous for its industrial pollution and illegal toxic waste dumps that over the years have caused genetic malformations in inhabitants, animals and plants alike. Before the National Park was founded on 1987, the Juréia was threatened on various occasions. In the early Seventies, for example, Praia do Rio Verde, one of the loveliest beaches in the area, was nearly destroyed by a huge holiday resort. A few years later, in 1980, during the atomic power boom, the President, General João Batista Figueredo, authorised the compulsory purchase of 236 square kilometres of land to build a nuclear power station; fortunately his plans came to nothing, because the project attracted neither funds nor support. Perhaps because of these precedents, it is very difficult to enter the Juréia park nowadays; visits by tourists are prohibited, and access is strictly limited to researchers and scientists.

In addition to the infinitely large Amazonia, the Pantanal and the Mata Atlântica, the gigantic Brazil contains a seemingly infinite amount of wildlife as a result of particular microclimates. For example, the Serra do Cipó National Park in Minas Gerais State contains the highest density of plants per square metre in the world; there are nearly 1,600 classified species (and researchers believe that a similar number still remain to be discovered) which flower all year round, continually transforming the landscape. Further south, towards the Argentinean border, dolphins and sealions, which arrive punctually every year to escape the Antarctic winter, play under the huge cliffs of Torres, a famous holiday resort in Rio Grande do Sul, which resemble the White Cliffs of Dover.

Hundreds of kilometres further north, in the State of Bahia, other great marine mammals gather every year to mate; these are whales, which have chosen to procreate and rear their young on the coast of Abrolhos. The name Abrolhos is a contraction of the phrase "Abra los olhos" (keep your eyes peeled). This is what sailors used to say when they ventured this way, as they kept a lookout for the coral reefs called *cabeças*, or heads – impressive towers that rise up suddenly from the sea bed to a height of 20 or 30 metres, on which a ship can run aground. The archipelago, which consists of four main islands (Santa Barbara, Sueste, Redonda and Guarita), was declared a National Marine Park in 1983.

58-59 Geography in Brazil is highly rich. Besides the vast plains, such as the Amazon basin and Pantanal, the vast South American country has mountains, deep valleys and plateaux. An example of this very great landscape variety is represented by Visconde de Mauá, a small town in the state of Rio de Janeiro.

59 top The Parque Nacional da Serra da Capivara, in the state of Piauí, has been placed under Unesco protection. Twenty years ago the Brazilian archaeologist Niéde Guidon discovered cave drawings and artefacts 48,500 years old. So far 363 archaeological sites have been opened in the Serra da Capivara.

60-61 Morro de São Paulo, 110 miles south of Salvador da Bahia, is one of the latest discoveries of international tourism. The tranquil fishing village has been flanked by resorts and hotels that are gambling all on this still uncontaminated corner of paradise. The splendid beach overlooks the 16 islands of the federal district of Valença.

62-63 Of volcanic origin, these small islands just 10 square miles in all are ideal for turtles and the numerous fish species that live in the rocky crevices. Fernando de Noronha, the main island and the only one inhabited, is open only to organized tours. A limited number of visitors are allowed at a time to avoid harming the delicate natural equilibrium.

63 top The Abrolhos archipelago, in the state of Bahia, like Fernando de Noronha, is a great paradise of nature, protected by a marine park. The whales of the Antarctic come to these warm waters to mate and spend the winter. In fact these islands attracted Charles Darwin in 1832 and,

much later, the oceanographer Jacques Cousteau intent on studying an unusual coral, called "brain" because of a remarkable resemblance to the human organ. The archipelago's five islands, of volcanic origin, are six hours by boat from the small town of Caravelas.

62 The Fernando de Noronha archipelago lies a few hundred miles from the coast of Brazil in the Atlantic Ocean. In 1988 it became a marine park spread over 42 square miles and it is in the state of Pernambuco. It was an American military base, then a gaol for political prisoners under the military dictatorship, but nature is now in charge here.

Other islands off the Brazilian coast, namely Fernando di Noronha and Trindade, have also been declared National Parks. Fernando di Noronha is now a sophisticated resort; only a limited number of people are allowed on the island at any one time, and to ensure that the right kind of tourist is attracted, package deal prices are not cheap. The first somewhat overawed tourists, who flew from Vinha do Recife to Noronha in a military aircraft on 7th December 1972, were able to discover this Brazilian land situated over 300 kilometres from the coast as a result of the nationalist policies pursued by the military dictatorship during the expansionist campaign. Having served as an American base during the Second World War and then a penal colony to which political prisoners were deported under the military dictatorship, the Fernando de Noronha Archipelago is now a strictly protected marine oasis owned by the State of Pernambuco. These breathtakingly beautiful islands, which have a total area of 26 square kilometres, were discovered by Amerigo Vespucci in 1503. The 17 beaches of Fernando de Noronha, the main island, are reflected in a crystal-clear sea. The National Park created in 1988 includes the sea as well as the islands, making a total area of 112 square kilometres. The scientists employed by the Tamar project, an agency that protects and studies turtles, work here. That's why tourists have to observe some very strict rules; those who harm the

wildlife on the archipelago are liable to expulsion. After years of neglect by man (goats were introduced and ruined the vegetation; huge lizards called teju were imported to get rid of rats, but preferred daintier fare such as turtles' eggs and birds), Fernando de Noronha is now a model for environmental protection projects in Brazil. The same applies to Trindade, the last outpost of Brazilian territory in the Atlantic, which lies 1,200 kilometres off the coast of the State of Espirito Santo. The island, of volcanic origin, is situated at the far end of an underwater mountain range that starts on the coast of Espirito Santo and ends at Trindade. Like Fernando de Noronha it has been a garrison (in the First and Second World Wars) and a penal colony. Since 1957 it has belonged to the Brazilian Navy, and is inhabited by around 30 men who supervise the passage of ships and work in a meteorological centre. Most civilians authorised to stay on the island are scientists working on the Tamar project.

Trindade is a major centre for turtles, especially the green turtle, now very rare, which makes 2-metre diameter holes in the beach to lay its eggs in. Another interesting sight on Trindade is the astonishing giant ferns, which can grow to a height of 6 metres. For years these huge plants have been a mystery to botanists, who are unable to explain their origin. Perhaps they grew from ancient Jurassic spores, carried here on the Atlantic currents millions of years ago.

CITIES SNATCHED FROM THE JUNGLE

RIO DE JANEIRO, MORE THAN A MYTH

64-65 This aerial view shows Ipanema and Leblon beaches in Rio de Janeiro. A road, running alongside the beaches, links the Barra, the new residential district, to the centre.

64 top left A cable car carries tourists to the top of Pao de Açúcar. From the summit the view sweeps the Corcovado, right opposite, and the whole metropolis and the morros, the hills that surround it.

64 top right The strip of sand called Leblon, the beach that lies just past Ipanema in the direction of Lagoa, is known for the Morro Pico Dois, a hill with two peaks.

65 Again an aerial view on the beaches of Rio where not only will tourists but the Cariocas strip off their clothes and spend some time on the beach, perhaps just for a game of beach volley or half an hour in the sun, during their lunch breaks or at the end of the day.

T he 30-metre tall Christ the Redeemer, anchored firmly on the top of the Corcovado, smiles beatifically down, arms outstretched towards Guanabara Bay and Pão de Açúcar (Sugar Loaf Mountain). This is the most famous picture-postcard view in Brazil. The impressive stone and marble statue, donated by the French and consecrated with full honours of Church and State in 1931, during the dictatorship of Getúlio Vargas, has seen a great deal from up there. From the summit, Rio de Janeiro looks like a quiet, magical, inoffensive city, with its clear blue sea, the long bridge connecting it to Niteroi, the strips of sandy beach and the skyscrapers, acting as a dividing line between the sea and the mountain. At the bottom is Avenida Vieira Souto which runs along Ipanema, then Lagoa, São Conrado, the tunnel, and the Barra, the new Rio for the rich. The wind that blows on the Corcovado prevents any noise from reaching it. Rio is always bewitching from up here. It's reminiscent of a lovely girl lying in a languid, sinuous, provocative pose. And like the classic femme fatale, it's dangerous. Between 1985 and 1991 there were 70,000 violent deaths in Rio, the same as the number of marines killed in Vietnam in 7 years of war. The magic of one of the loveliest cities in the world risks being ruined when you walk along its streets. The people here are frightened; they live in fear

of being robbed, or killed for a few coins. This anxiety is so strong that it is also communicated to tourists. But that's the way it goes. You can't ask too much of a city with over 12 million inhabitants, a third of whom live in the *favelas*. Poverty and social inequality are rife. Murders of street children are commonplace, as are shoot-outs between rival drug-dealing gangs. Two tons of cocaine a month are consumed, amounting to a turnover of 20 million dollars. Yet despite this terrible picture, which would suggest that a self-imposed curfew is advisable, the citizens of Rio (known as *Cariocas*), still risk violence and fear to go out on warm tropical nights. The city's night life is enlivened by local character Ricardo Amarao, Italian on his

66 bottom
The beaches of Copacabana, Ipanema, Leblon, São Conrado and now the Barra have made Rio de Janeiro famous. The Cariocas, as the inhabitants of Rio are known, live in

virtual symbiosis with the sand and sea - like the surfers who face the breakers of the Baía de Guanabara, heedless of the swimming ban signalled on many of the beaches for the high pollution levels.

67 Sexual tourism, predominantly male, has brought major income to the hotels and restaurants of Rio. Americans and Italians, with Germans and Japanese, only represent the majority of customers. Today,

with the public campaigns promoted all over the country by Embratur, the Brazilian Ministry of Tourism, the pleasure seekers have left Rio only to move north to Recife and Fortaleza.

66 top The best hotels also stand along the crowded beaches of Rio - the mythical Copacabana Palace, the Othon and the Caesar Park. Besides the beach and the calzadão, *the black and white tiled pavement, the main rendezvous, the city has numerous monuments dating from colonial and modernist times.*

66 centre Although not expressly banned, hardly any Brazilian women go topless. Breasts may be covered but not so the bumbum, *the delightful name given to the buttocks, which must preferably be left bare: the* fil dental, *dental floss - the tiniest of bikinis - was invented on these very beaches.*

grandparents' side from the province of Treviso. This former journalist, who was unpopular under the dictatorship, is now a wealthy impresario, with music bars and discos in every city of Brazil, and even in New York.

Rio is not only the birthplace of the samba and carnival; culture and fashions are invented there, successful bands are formed there and actors, singers and authors live there. One reason is that the city of the Sugar Loaf Mountain is also the headquarters of Rede Globo, the most famous television network in Latin America. Roberto Marinho, its octogenarian owner, is the most powerful man in the country; he creates and destroys political careers, decides who gets to be President of the Republic, supports one candidate and ruins another. That's the power of South American soaps for you. Although Rio has not been the capital of Brazil for nearly 40 years, the beautiful, provocative Brazilian city still acts if it were – for better or worse. It mirrors the South American giant and the love of all things Brazilian, from the samba to futebol. Apart from dancing, soccer is the all-consuming passion of the Cariocas. Imported by an Englishman in 1894, the game of bola was perfected to the extent that it became the country's top sport. Going to the legendary Maracaná stadium is like entering a church; everything is sacred, from the chair

where Pelé used to get changed to Zico's jacuzzi and Garrincha's massage couch. Fetishism and iconoclasm are rife in the great stadium, which can hold almost 200,000 spectators. The walls are covered with photos of the stars who made the Brazilian team great: Rivelino, Junior, Zico, Garrincha, Romario and, of course, *o rei* (the King) Pelé, who is now Minister of Sport. Apart from Garrincha, who died an alcoholic, forgotten by fans and friends alike, they have all made the most of the huge fortunes they have accumulated. Artur Antunes Coimbra Zico has opened a football school in the Barra, and teaches the courses himself; Rivelino operates numerous junior football pitches in São Paolo, while Junior is a talent scout for the selectors and plays footvolley, a cross between football and beach volleyball, on the beach at Barra, in front of his house.

The beach is the common denominator of the city. The residents play, stroll and make friends by the sea. At least once a day, early in the morning (rarely), during the lunch break or at the end of the day, Copacabana, Ipanema, Leblon and São Conrado fill with people. They sunbathe, have something to eat at the kiosks or swim, despite the "no bathing" notices all over the place. The beach is a way of life; it enables the Cariocas to have fun without spending much money, and enhances their reputation as unenthusiastic workers.

68-69 *Corcovado, the mountain with the statue of Christ the Redeemer, has one of the loveliest sunsets over the Baía de Guanabara. The top can be reached by car, passing through the Floresta da Tijuca, or on a cog train.*

68 top *Although Rio de Janeiro has lost 30 % of its tourism as a result of violence due to drug trafficking and poverty, it is still the most popular city in Brazil with tourists, and more than 45% of the visitors come here.*

They're all deeply sun-tanned and at the peak of fitness, because if you're going to show off your body, it ought to be presentable. As they spend much of their time in a bikini or swimming trunks they can't rely on stratagems to improve their appearance. This may be why the college for plastic surgeons (who have Ivo Pitanguy as their guru and predecessor) is the most famous in the world. In any event, they all try to keep their figures with a healthy diet: big salads, not much meat, brown rice, fish and plenty of fruit juice. Their diet always includes iced beer, a concession which everyone makes, whether they are fat or thin, dieting or in great shape. The tourists who flock to the beaches and the five-star hotels also get caught up in the beach life. As a result, by the end of their trip the vast majority know only their own hotel room, the beach and a few night clubs. Few tourists realise that one of the best collections of modernist buildings in Latin America is hidden away in the oldest part of what was once the capital of Brazil. Nor do they know that the city centre Prefecture has devised an itinerary called the Corredor Cultural, a walk through the architecture of an unusual Rio, which nonchalantly passes from the beautiful colonial style of the Paço Imperial (the Emperor's Palace) to Cinêlandia (the modernist district where the city's cinemas were built), from Confeitaria Colombo (a magnificent Art Nou-

veau building where hundreds of valuable glasses are displayed in the tall cases surrounding the bar) to the conical modern cathedral, and from the arched aqueduct, where trams now run, to the Municipal Theatre, built at the turn of the century in the style of the Paris Opera House.

Even the Rocinha, the most famous of the 600 *favelas* situated on the hillsides around the city, has its own architectural style. It has now become a city within a city; buses run there, every home has water and electricity, and the colourful houses, seen from a distance, look like an Impressionist painting. The Rio of the poor, for decades the symbol of total poverty, is getting its own back; in view of its location, which gives a beautiful view of the city, it is now much sought after. The inhabitants are well aware of this, and anyone wanting to buy a house here has to pay a high price for it – at city centre prices.

69 Rocinha is the most densely-populated favela in Rio de Janeiro. Seen from afar it resembles an Impressionist painting - the brick houses are patches of colour that blend together. The favela is a city within a city: it has more than half a million inhabitants, an internal bus service, electricity and water.

THE METROPOLITAN CONTRADICTIONS OF SÃO PAULO

70-71 The circular Hotel Hilton skyscraper is one of the numerous and most modern skyscrapers in São Paolo and can be admired from the panoramic terrace of the Edifício Itália, the tallest building in the historic centre.

70 top left Dom Pedro I declared the independence of Brazil from Portugal in 1822 on the spot where the Museo Ipiranga now stands. Built in neoclassical style it houses objects that belonged to the royal family as well as the famous painting O Grito Ipiranga portraying Dom Pedro I crying "Independence or death".

70 top right The Bandeiras *monument stands in the Parque Ibirapuera, the large park of São Paulo. The* bandeirantes, *flag wavers, originated here in São Paulo, pioneers who joined together under the same flag to seek gold, capture slaves and build new towns.*

71 The Sé is the modern cathedral of São Paulo dating from the beginning of the century. The square of the same name, entirely shaded by majestic trees, is where the street children live and is one of the most dangerous parts of the city.

All the faces of the city can be seen along the Marginal Pinheiros, the orbital motorway which, together with the Tieté, encircles São Paolo. Ultramodern skyscrapers, large shopping centres, residential complexes, even the World Trade Centre. Then suddenly, as if the future had been swallowed up by the exhaust fumes of millions of vehicles, the *favelas* appear – shacks of cardboard and sheet metal that cover the natural undulations of the land. Behind them are more skyscrapers, those of Morumbí, one of the most fashionable and expensive districts of the city, where each apartment has its own private swimming pool. The road continues with the alternation of opulence and poverty so typical of Brazil, interrupted by small blocks of new council flats; this is the Singapura project, a facelift operation ordered by Paulo Maluf, former mayor of the city. Eliminating the awful cardboard shacks, giving a home to the homeless and introducing a semblance of cleanliness and decency, the project was one of the priorities of his administration.

Expressing an opinion about São Paolo, the largest city in Latin America and second-largest in the world after Mexico City in terms of population, is a difficult task. At first sight, when you begin to see the endless stretch of houses, skyscrapers and *favelas* followed by more houses, skyscrapers and *favelas* from the win-

dows of the plane or the roof of the Edifício Itália, the tallest skyscraper in the city, built by Italians, your opinion is bound to be unfavourable. It just looks like a jumble of buildings with no town planning, no shape, nothing. Then, as you start to get used to the city, you discover that all this chaos is actually an age-old order that cannot be altered, even to a small extent. You realise then that the Brazilian metropolis is not a single city, but a group of towns, large and small, and that there is no single dominant culture (as in Salvador, where African culture predominates) but a number of cultures – the city is inhabited by Italians, Japanese, Lithuanians and Arabs.

Going to Bixiga or Moca, the Italian districts, is nothing like entering the streets of Liberdade, the nearby Japanese district. There, red archways welcome visitors, and bilingual wording (in Japanese and Portuguese) on the products sold in the

shops and restaurant menus is common practice. The original cultures are manifested in the street décor, food and cafés, as well as in the language. The festival of Nossa Senhora da Aquiropita, the Madonna who protects Bixiga, in the second week of August, is well worth seeing (this period is winter time, and because of its geographical position, the temperature in São Paolo often falls to as little as 3 or 4 degrees); colourful stalls flying Italian flags sell pizza, lasagna, pasta and sandwiches filled with calabreza, a spicy sausage, all washed down with mulled wine.

What really makes São Paolo is the people who live there. According to IBGE (the Institute of Statistical Geography) there are 16.5 million of them, not counting those who arrive every day in search of work and end up by swelling the population of the *favelas*. As many as 19-20 million people are said to live in the metropolitan district of São Paolo, and it's not hard to believe. The neighbouring towns no longer exist; they've been swallowed up by the inexorable advance of the capital. There are never enough roads; they disappear under the Pinheiros River then climb to a viaduct and cross the river from the other side; *favelas* are razed to the ground and new by-passes opened to relieve the perennial gridlock along the 100 kilometre route connecting one side of the city to the other.

In the middle of all these roads,

72 top Santos is the port that serves São Paulo. Roughly 40 miles from the metropolis, this is where all the European immigrants landed at the beginning of the century. Despite being a modern city, Santos still preserves some valuable colonial masterpieces such as the Mosteiro de São Benito founded in 1649 and the Carmelite convent with the Igreja de Nossa Senhora do Carmo of 1589.

72 bottom Landmarks in the centre of São Paulo are the Martinelli building, the first 30-storey skyscraper in Latin America built by the Italians in 1915, and the Banespa, the bank of São Paulo which resembles the Empire State Building in New York.

near Ibirapuera Park in the southern part of town, stands a Formula One car. The stylised bronze vehicle, flying a flag, commemorates the victories of Ayrton Senna, the unforgettable racing driver from São Paolo. The tunnel under the obelisk erected to commemorate the martyrs of the 1932 revolution is named after him. Ibirapuera Park is the largest park in the city. Designed by world-famous landscape gardener Roberto Burle-Marx, it's the meeting place for all the inhabitants of São Paolo; they flock there to eat ice-cream, jog, sunbathe, admire the Japanese garden and watch the blue herons lazily looking at their reflections in the great lake. Those lucky enough to live near the park are sitting on a goldmine; building is now prohibited in the area, and the skyscrapers built on the tiny spaces available (the land is exploited to the full) look threateningly down on the huge villas surrounding this paradise on earth.

The city centre, Praça da Sé (the cathedral square) is just the opposite of Ibirapuera. This is São Paolo at its noisiest and most irreverent. It attracts all sorts: the poor, street children who bathe in the fountain built above the subway, *camelô* (hawkers who sell strange potions), painters and former hippies all flock here and to the nearby Praça da República to sell their home-made products. The pews in the cathedral serve as beds for the poor. A service

72-73 São Paulo is a vast metropolis. It measures 37 miles from north to south and the same from east to west. The exact number of inhabitants is unknown but they are thought to be more than 15,000,000 people, 10 per cent of the national population.

73 top Every weekend the Paulistanos move to the beaches of Guarujá, a seaside resort 60 miles north of Sao Paulo. The litoral norte, of which Guarujá is a part, is one of the most beautiful coastlines in Brazil.

in the great church is like something out of a Fellini film. The priest sings and dances to the rhythm of the music and the congregation follow his lead, while an army of children, adults and old people sleep stretched out on the pews or doze behind the great columns, their few pathetic rags done up in a bundle.

Light years separate these everyday scenes from Avenida Paulista, the best-known thoroughfare in the city. This is the financial centre of São Paolo, where skyscrapers designed by world-famous architects symbolise the opulence of what seems like a different city. Halfway along the Avenida is the Rede Globo receiving tower, which looks like a miniature Eiffel Tower at night. Then there are the Fiat building and the MASP (Art Museum), designed by the Italian architect Lina Bo Bardi and her husband Pietro Maria Bardi, a leading art expert and collector, who has put together one of the most interesting permanent exhibitions in the world.

Yet another face of the metropolis is art and culture, which live in the Memorial da América Latina (a huge arts complex containing libraries, museums and a theatre, all built by Oscár Niemeyer), the Municipal Theatre and the University, which has its own mayor who ministers to the continual needs of the huge American-style campus.

São Paolo never ceases to amaze the visitor. While Rio, with its legendary beaches, has remained unchanged for years, and Bahia lives on candomblé, magic and colonial buildings, São Paolo is the symbol of change, the metronome beating out the rhythm of this young country's growth.

This is perhaps the only way that the gigantic metropolis can convey to the inexpert eyes of the visitor something other than concrete, pollution and contradictions.

74-75 The obelisk-mausoleum in front of the Parque Ibirapuera was built to commemorate those who died during the 1932 civil war. They were members of the 1932 constitutionalist movement which wanted the authoritarian Vargas to introduce democratic rules and were supported by the Paulistanos alone after Rio de Janeiro, Minas Gerais and Rio Grande do Sul, who had initially adhered, decided to support the president Getúlio, elected with their consent.

75 top The Vale do Anhangabaú is a major road junction with tunnels that connect the south and the north of the metropolis. There is an excellent view of it from the viaduct of the same name built in the late Twenties.

SALVADOR, THE CALL OF MOTHER AFRICA

*T*oday, like every Tuesday, is *o dia da bensa* (the Day of Benediction). The service is held at 6 p.m. at the Cathedral of São Francisco. After Mass the celebrating monk blesses the congregation, numerous as ever, gathered in the golden baroque shadows of the most famous church in Salvador, capital of the State of Bahia. Everyone attends the service: children and adults, rich and poor, and the sick, huddled on wheelchairs or leaning on improvised crutches. The time of devotion and meditation ends with the sign of the cross. Immediately after the prayer, the fun begins. The Pelourinho (the largest colonial city centre in South America, which is protected by Unesco) is closed to traffic, and the population throng the streets, drinking beer, chatting, dancing and playing instruments until late into the night. The Day of Benediction is just a pretext, because in the Pelô (as the Bahians affectionately call the Pelourinho), as in the rest of the city, even the smallest event becomes an opportunity for amusement. Up and down the streets they go, laughing and dancing, talking and listening. In recent years, only the backdrop has changed. The old buildings, inhabited first by Portuguese noblemen and later by the homeless poor, were falling to pieces, and have now been renovated by degrees, and restored to their original splendour. This facelift was ordered by Antônio Carlos Magalhães, former Governor of the State of Bahia and one of the most influential politicians in Brazil. The result is astonishing to anyone who has been able to compare the two faces of the Pelourinho, before and after its renovation, although (as frequently occurs) the city centre has been emptied of ordinary people to make way for shops, restaurants and jewellers, all for tourists. However, the inhabitants of Salvador still come up here to chat, listen to music, and sit in the cafés or simply in front of the Amado Foundation in Largo do Pelourinho. Here in Salvador there is a saying that every day God sends is a festival, and it's not hard to believe if you take a look at the city. With its baroque churches dedicated to Christian saints and its *terreiros di candomblé* (areas consecrated to African deities), the first capital of colonial Brazil is the repository of the Brazilian religions, so it comes as no surprise to find that any anniversary is celebrated with devotion. The African soul, forcibly deported on slave ships until the 19th century, has taken its revenge here in Salvador; the majority of the population are black, and the rest are mulattos. "Is there a white man, even the whitest of the whites, who does not have some black blood in his blue veins? Doesn't the blackest black man also have a drop of white blood in his African veins?" wondered author Jorge Amado, the bard and symbol of Bahia. The mixture of races has created the "pure, unrivalled beauty of the Cape Verde mulattos, creatures out of a dream, a dream of love", concludes the elderly author in his dissertation on the origins of the Bahians. And you

78-79
The Pelourinho is the colonial city centre of Salvador da Bahia. Nominated a World Heritage site, it can now be admired in all its splendour thanks to careful restoration started in 1992. More than 50 million dollars, all provided by the Bahian government, have been spent so far to restore this colonial monument.

can't argue with him. You only need to take a walk through the streets of the city, sprawling over the mountainside, to see and understand. From the Pelourinho to the areas higher up, where houses give way to shanties, the African culture of *candomblé*, with the Yoruba deities Olodum, Oxum and Oxossí, Axé and Oxalá, is part of everyday life. Wherever you go, to the seaside, to the Mercado Modelo (the forerunner of the shopping centre, where you can find absolutely anything), or to the new part of town, among the inevitable skyscrapers of a continually changing country, the African deities live and breathe. The full name of the city is Cidade de Salvador de Bahia de Todos os Santos (City of Salvador in Bahia of All Saints). *Pai de santo* (candomblé priest) Jubiabá, the hero of Jorge Amado's novel of the same name, inevitably comes to mind (there's even a square in the Pelourinho named after him). Very old, black as coal, dried up and incredibly thin, enveloped in a gown that fluttered like a flag in the ocean breeze, at his house in Morro de Capa Negro, on the mountain above Salvador, Jubiabá saw into everyone's soul, read the good and evil there, helped and cured. Salvador bowed to his wisdom. Another famous character, this time historical rather than literary, was Mãe Menininha, the famous *mãe de santo* (candomblé priestess). She was consulted by politicians and artists, and was so famous that people came from all over Brazil to ask her for help and advice. The people of Salvador also

remember Irmã Doce, an elderly nun who, like Mother Teresa of Calcutta, founded hospitals and assistance posts for the poor. These are the personalities of Bahia, present-day saints who join the ranks of those of centuries ago, laid to rest in the baroque church. Yoruba saints are also venerated in the Catholic Church of Nossa Senhora do Rosario dos Pretos, in Largo do Pelourinho, where the last scene from the film "Dona Flor and her Two Husbands" was shot. Veneration and respect for the deities is matched by equal devotion to music and the arts in general. African rhythms originated in Salvador, as did Tropicalism, a historical movement of Brazilian musical culture in the Seventies, led by Caetano Veloso, Gilberto Gil and Gal Costa. Salvador is also the home of Axé music (a blend of the music of the Olodum and Timbalada tribes), the romantic dance music of Daniela Mercury (the grand-daughter of a Genoese couple who emigrated to Bahia), and the eclectic sounds of Carlinhos Brown. "The Americans had to build Disneyworld to have fun – Bahia was created like that", quips Daniela Mercury. And it's true; there's no lack of gaiety and love of celebration even among the poorest of the poor, who live in shanties by the sea or the *favelas* perched on the mountainside. Magic and fun, philosophy of life and tradition, Europe and Africa, the sacred and the profane. All this is found in Bahia, a great plaza on the emerald green ocean – the same ocean that gave birth to Salvador, City of All Saints and All Festivals.

OURO PRETO,
LEGENDS FROM
COLONIAL BRAZIL

Many people swear they have seen him at least once. In the Church of São Francisco de Assis, one of the most outstanding examples of colonial baroque, a hooded friar wearing a black cloak slowly walks and prays, his habit brushing against the solid wooden pews. If anyone tries to approach him, he vanishes. The ghost of the praying Franciscan is just one of those who glide undisturbed and disappear among the majestic walls of Ouro Preto, the ancient capital of Minas Gerais. Spirits and goblins, black and white, haunt the quiet nights of the ancient Vila Rica (its original name). Some shuffle around the churches like Maria Chinela (literally Mary Slipper), a little old black lady who used to stroll along the streets of Vila Rica many years ago, and is now satisfied with filling the Church of Nossa Senhora do Monte do Carmo with the sound of her shuffling footsteps. Others mourn their lost love in the cemeteries, like Bolão, an insensitive student who rejected his fiancée Emília; she died of a broken heart, and he was found dead on her grave. Some speak the African Yoruba language in the churchyard of Santa Efigênia, the place of worship of the slaves, who fooled the Jesuits and the Portuguese by hiding symbols of their own deities among the Christian symbols.

Others again attend evening mass, shrouded in black cloaks, before

80 top Ouro Preto is a university town, the home of one of the most prestigious mineralogy faculties in the world. The students live in repúblicas, *student-run houses on several storeys where visitors can stay and where students study, dance and socialize.*

80 bottom Praça Tiradentes is the main square of Ouro Preto and, being on the top of a hill, divides the town in two parts. In 1792 the head of Joaquim da Silva Xavier, the leader of the Inconfidentes who called for the independence of the state of Minas Gerais from Portugal, was hung here.

80-81 Ouro Preto is situated on a mine of precious stones: aquamarine, imperial topaz and emeralds. Stone-cutting and setting have provided the town with its major source of income since 1750 when this colonial gem had more inhabitants than New York.

81 São Francisco de Paula was the last church built at Ouro Preto; work ended at the beginning of this century. It stands in a privileged position at the top of a hill overlooking the lovely colonial city of Minas Gerais.

82-83 The church of Carmo, the work of Aleijadinho and his father, Manoel Francisco Lisboa, is marked by the absence of sumptuous and overwhelming baroque decorations. There is no excess here: only harmony and lucidity of thought. The church is part of the third and last phase of Mineiro baroque style.

82 top Chafariz (fountains) are a common sight in the streets of Ouro Preto. In 1980 the town was placed under Unesco protection, and quite rightly so - at every turn there is a work of art to stimulate the curiosity of the visitor.

returning to their tombs, as once happened on a dark rainy night at the Church of Nossa Senhora das Mercês e Misericórdia. All this coming and going of ghosts and zombies is enough to terrify even the most sceptical of visitors.

Whether the stories are true or false, one thing's for sure: Ouro Preto, a town nestling at the foot of Pico de Itacolomí, a mountain that resembles a bent old Indian woman, really does have something special; religion blends with animist cults, popular beliefs with the sacred places, and solemn buildings with the cheerful din made by students enrolled at one of the most famous universities in Latin America.

Gold, imperial topazes, emeralds, aquamarines and rubies have made Ouro Preto a fabulously wealthy city; in 1750 it had more inhabitants than New York. In just over a century, between 1700 and 1820, some 1,200 tons of gold were mined in the State of Minas Gerais, accounting for 80% of world gold production. Ouro Preto was the hub of mining activities.

The chronicles of the period recount that even the slaves were dressed in gold. One of them, Chico Rei, an African sovereign deported with his whole tribe in the early 18th century to work in the mines, became a legend. It is not known whether he really existed, but the story goes that by hiding gold dust in his hair, he managed to accumulate such wealth

that he was able to buy freedom for his whole tribe and purchase a mine, Encardideira, which the Portuguese believed to be worked out. Chico was lucky enough to strike a new gold seam which made him a rich and powerful man.

To thank Efigênia, the Christian Nubian princess who was the patron saint of the tribe, he built a church named after her. A commemorative mass was celebrated on 6th January for many years. On that occasion the negro women sprinkled gold dust on their heads, and rinsed their hair in holy water after the service, thus contributing to the maintenance of the place of worship.

The saying that Ouro Preto has more churches than houses is not entirely wrong. It may be exaggerated, but 13 churches and 6 chapels in one small town is certainly no mean figure. These places of worship were built in the golden years of the 18th century, when rich men and aristocrats vied to erect the most magnificent building under pressure from the Jesuits, who admired baroque art. The last *igreja* (church) to be built was the Church of São Francisco de Paula, which was started in 1804 and was finished exactly a century later. As regards non-religious buildings, the only recent construction in the city centre is a hotel built in the Sixties by architect Oscár Niemeyer. The all-concrete building is a fine example of "new style" design, but somewhat out of place.

83 top São Francisco de Assís is perhaps the most outstanding work of Antônio Francisco Lisboa, the architect and sculptor responsible for most of the monuments in Minas Gerais.

83 bottom Inside the church of São Francisco de Assís are paintings by Manoel da Costa Ataíde, one of the leading Brazilian painters. Ataíde worked on the church from 1801 to 1812.

84-85 The sanctuary
of Senhor Bom Jesus
de Matozinhos is the
main attraction in
Congonhas do Campos.
Except for this baroque
religious complex the
town remains fairly
anonymous.

84 top left
The imprisonment of
Christ is again by
Aleijadinho, a
nickname which in
Portuguese means
"little cripple". The
artist suffered from
severe deforming
arthritis and for this
reason hid his body
beneath a large cloak.
Towards the end of his
life, to continue
sculpting, he had to have
the hammer and chisel
strapped to his hands.

84 top right
Sixty wooden statues
make up the Way of
the Cross in small
chapels in front of
the sanctuary of
Congonhonas do
Campos.
That of the
suffering Christ
with almond-shaped
eyes and mouth
half-open in a
grimace of pain is
perhaps the loveliest.
All are the work of
Aleijadinho.

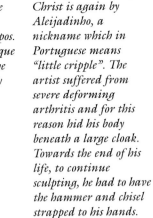

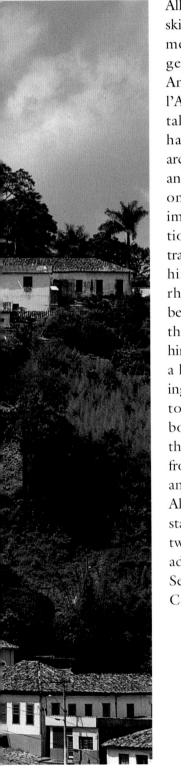

All this opulence was entrusted to the skilful hands of carpenters and craftsmen, working to the orders of a genius of church architecture, Antônio Francisco Lisboa, known as l'Aleijadinho (the little cripple). Many tales are told about this illegitimate half-caste, the son of Portuguese architect Manuel Francisco Lisboa and an African slave called Isabel. But the one which has made the greatest impression on the popular imagination was the serious disease he contracted at the age of 47, which turned him into a cripple. The disease was rheumatoid arthritis, and his body became horribly twisted. To hide from the eyes of people who remembered him as a dashing young man, he wore a large black cloak with a hood. During the last period of his life he is said to have had a hammer and chisel bound to the stumps of his arms so that he could keep on carving. Apart from designing São Francisco de Assis and many other churches in the city, Aleijadinho left a series of magnificent statues in Minas Gerais, especially the twelve Old Testament prophets who adorn the façade of the Sanctuary of Senhor Bom Jesus de Matozinhos at Congonhas do Campo (Isaiah, the

first on the left, small and bent with a pain-racked face, is none other than the artist himself) and the capitals of the Via Crucis, resembling life-sized theatre sets, in the same place. Antônio Francisco Lisboa hated the Portuguese, regarded as invaders, as did all the intelligentsia of Minas Gerais (Ouro Preto was the centre of the *Inconfidentes* conspiracy led by Tiradentes). The ideal weapon to fight and denigrate the Portuguese was Aleijadinho's chisel. All his statues representing treacherous or evil characters were ugly portraits of Portuguese personalities. One example is the statue of São Jorge, housed in the city's museum. Aleijadinho resented the fact that Bernardo José Lorena, the Portuguese governor who commissioned him to carve a statue of St. George, had looked at his horribly deformed body with disgust, and decided to take his revenge. He gave the saint the features of the nobleman's servant, accentuating his physical defects and intentionally botching the proportion between torso and legs. The result was that for many years, instead of ending with prayers and devotion, the procession of São Jorge degenerated into general hilarity.

85 top The prophet
Isaiah is one of the 12
soapstone statues that
adorn the dual
stairway of the church
of Senhor Bom Jesus
do Matosinhos in
Congonhas do Campo.
Experts believe that

Isaiah is a self-
portrait of
Aleijadinho himself.
The statues,
threatened by the
atmospheric pollution
that was slowly
eroding them, have
recently been restored.

85 bottom Also the
statue of prophet
Ezekiel stands on the
stairway of the church
of Senhor Bom Jesus.
The religious complex
features an unusual
Way of the Cross by
Aleijadinho.

BRASILIA, AN IMPOSSIBLE DREAM

A red cloud shrouds the blue sky above the city. It's a dust cloud, formed by the classic blood-red soil of Brazil, stirred up by the wind. This phenomenon occurs frequently in winter, when the humidity level can drop to as little as 18-20%. We're in the wild Planalto Central, situated at an altitude of 1,100 metres in the State of Goiás, precisely at the geographical centre of Brazil. 37 years ago, this godforsaken spot was chosen as the birthplace of a city, or rather the city – Brasilia, the capital, the first 20th-century metropolis to be built from scratch. The impressive project was designed by three famous names of modern architecture: town planner Lúcio Costa, architect Oscár Niemeyer, and landscape gardener Roberto Burle-Marx. Brasilia was the first modern city to be classed by Unesco as a "heritage of the human race". "*A arquitetura deve ser uma manifestação do espírito, da imaginação e da poesia*" ("architecture should be a manifestation of spirit, imagination and poetry"), said Niemeyer when Brasilia took shape. The new architectural style, which was daring and futuristic in the Fifties and Sixties, had already been used for the Education Ministry Building in Rio de Janeiro, the first building designed by the trio, which acted as their reference for the building of Brasilia. Despite their real artistic and innovative merits, the new designs did not produce a very functional city; in fact, Niemeyer himself admitted that the needs of sophisticated planning and structural studies took precedence over the convenience of residents. The identical blocks recall the depressing buildings of Communist countries, the streets have numbers instead of names, and all that concrete gets oppressive in the long run. Nevertheless the capital, which was designed to house 400,000 people, now has a population of 1,750,000. Many of them, especially the *candangos* (the pioneers who built Brasilia) now live outside the city, in *favelas* that stretch as far as 30 kilometres from Plano Piloto, the original structure of the project. The other residents, nearly all of them civil servants working for ministries or government agencies, live in low-rise buildings or pretty villas on the lakeside, the residential area. Brasilia has a fluctuating population; it is overcrowded from Monday to Thursday and deserted at weekends, when members of Congress, secretaries, bag-carriers and civil servants go back to their home towns. Those who can't afford the flight every weekend flock to private clubs out of town. It was very difficult to populate the new capital. Forty years ago, to persuade civil servants and politicians to leave Rio de Janeiro, one of the most fascinating cities in Latin America, Juscelino Kubitschek appealed to their wallets, doubling their salaries. Now, 37 years later, more and more people love to live in this strange city, a work of art that belongs to "a different planet, not the earth", as astronaut Yuri Gagarin commented when he visited it for the first time.

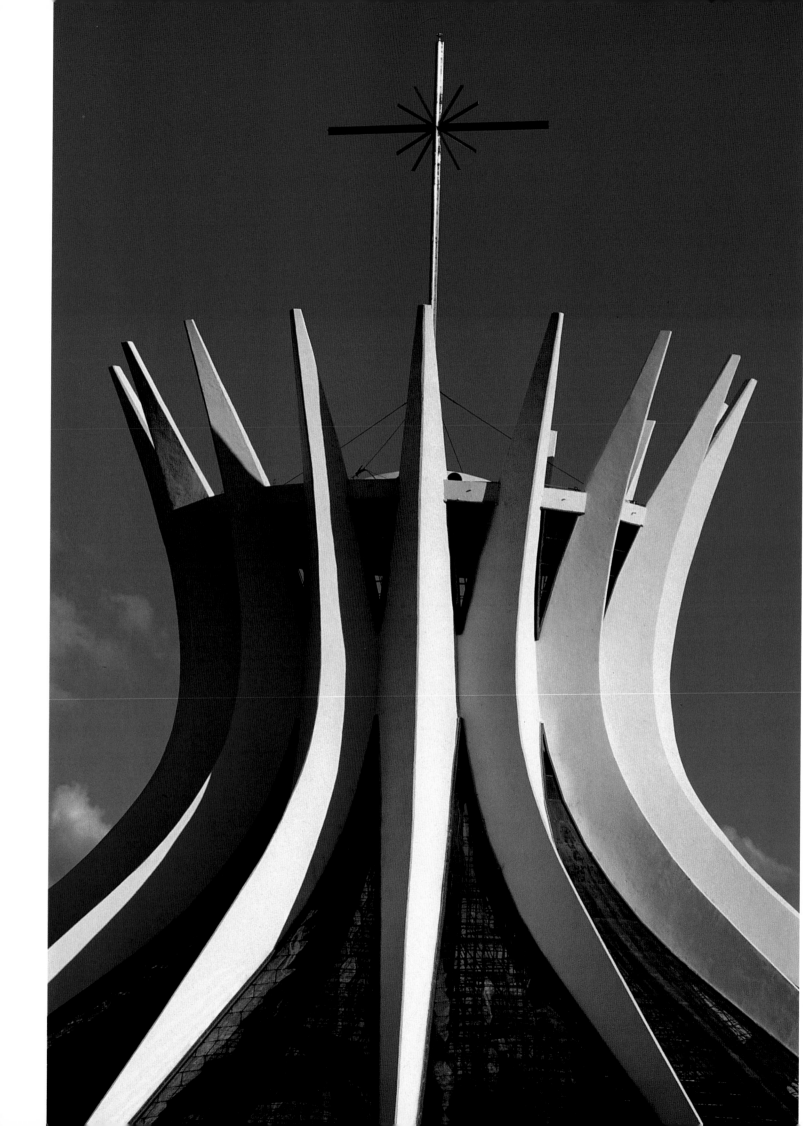

88 and 89
The Cathedral of Brasília is Niemeyer's greatest achievement, inaugurated in 1967 12 years after work commenced. Conceived as a universal place of worship, bringing together all the creeds in Brazil, in the end it was consecrated to Catholicism and named Catedral Metropolitana de Nossa Senhora Aparecida. Consisting of a single nave supported on external pillars, from above it looks like a flower (centre) covered with glass windows that create a play of light and colour inside. The entrance to this splendid modern church was designed as a journey of purification towards God: the doorway is in semi-darkness which as the visitor proceeds towards the central nave becomes gradually brighter before exploding at the main altar (bottom).

Brasilia is certainly a world apart. A world influenced by many factors, from the school which developed in São Paolo after Modern Art Week was held there in 1922 (Niemeyer was only 13 at the time) to the arrival of Le Corbusier in Rio de Janeiro in 1931. Le Corbusier, the king of modern architecture, gave a clear direction to the work of young Brazilian architects, including Costa, Niemeyer and Burle-Marx. Simple design, economical use of construction materials and large open spaces – these were the lessons of the French master, and the ideas which inspired the construction of Brasilia, city of the future, home of the arts and an exercise in style. The city does not merely represent the cold application of revolutionary tenets of style, but incorporates a compendium of Brazilian philosophy. From the layout of the town to the coldest of its buildings, everything has a meaning, a carefully designed symbolism. For example, the city is shaped like an aeroplane, with the Planalto (Presidential Palace) as the cockpit, signifying that this new city, where the political and administrative heart of the country beats, will lead Brazil to the future and a better world. The magnificent cathedral, one of the most famous monuments of the 20th century, is also imbued with symbolism. Niemeyer intended the cathedral, inaugurated in 1967 after 12 years' work, to be an ecumenical religious centre, a place of worship where all the Brazilian religions would be equally welcome: Brasilia, the democratic syn-

thesis of all the manifestations of the people. However, the place of worship was transformed into the Roman Catholic Catedral Metropolitana de Nossa Senhora Aparecida. The circular nave is situated below ground level; it is reached by walking through a tunnel with black walls and floor that gives onto a softly lit room, called the meditation area. After crossing this room you reach the central nave, which is illuminated by natural light filtering through the stained-glass windows forming the walls. The effect is that of a kind of Pilgrim's Progress before seeing the light – God.
The buildings housing the ministries in the wide Avenida named after them are all the same, standing guard over the power base situated at the end of the road in the Square of the Three Powers: the executive represented by the Planalto, the judiciary by the Law Courts, and the legislature by the twin towers of the National Congress. A slow, magnificent route towards the horizon, beyond which there seems to be nothing. On either side stand the most important ministries, the Ministry of the Interior and the Itamaraty (Foreign Ministry), a perfect harmony of concrete, green tropical plants and water cascading down the pillars of the façade to collect in a huge fountain. The same forms are encountered in other buildings by Niemeyer, from the French Communist Party building in Paris to the National University in Algiers, from the Mondadori building in Milan to the magnificent Church of

89

90-91 It was not easy to populate Brasília. The first to arrive were the employees of the various ministries, abruptly wrenched away from the beauties of Rio and thrown into a city that had nothing in common with the Cariocan beaches and nightlife. Salaries were increased to encourage transfers and even now, at weekends, the residents take refuge in clubs outside the city or in villas around the artificial lake of Paranoá.

90 top The Esplanada dos Ministerios is perhaps the most fascinating part of Brasília, ending with the Praça dos Tres Poderes. The capital, conceived for 400,000 people, today has 1,750,000 inhabitants. Many of these work in the ministries and spend just a few days of the week here, from Monday to Thursday.

São Francisco de Assis, frescoed by Italo-Brazilian artist Cândido Portinari, in Pampulha, Belo Horizonte (Minas Gerais).

Parks and gardens are another important feature of Brasilia, and Burle-Marx was commissioned to design them. The Parque da Cidade covers an area of 4,200,000 square metres. This huge park has absolutely everything, from cycle tracks to children's play areas, a lake you can fish in, and a swimming pool with artificial waves that can reach 1 metre high. There's also a huge indoor area covering 57,000 square metres, and an amphitheatre with a seating capacity of 1,400. Brasilia is an acquired taste. You learn to like it, or even love it for its new, simple yet complex forms. The best declaration of love for the city was expressed by Alçeu Valencia, a singer-songwriter from the North-East Region, and it is appropriate to close with his words on the story of Brasilia, new capital and white elephant of Planalto Central, Gioás, a city that is outside everything but at the centre of everything:

"Agora conheço tua geografia,
a pele macia, cidade menina,
teu sexo, teu lago teu simetria,
até qualquer dia te amo Brasilia."

"Now I know your geography,
your soft skin, girl city,
your sex, your lake, your symmetry.
See you soon, I love you, Brasilia."

91 top Brasília, today a federal district, is actually part of the state of Goiás. Construction work started in 1956 and the new city was inaugurated in 1961.

It lies in the geographical centre of Brazil, in a very dry, desert area where humidity can rise only to 15%. Often the sky is turned red, coloured by the dry earth raised by the wind.

91 bottom The monument to the candangos, the workers and natives who built Brasília, stands right in front of the Ministry of Justice. The candangos now live in favelas (shanty-towns) extending for up to 20 miles outside the Plano Piloto, the original nucleus of the city.

92-93 Curitiba -
an island in the vast
continent of South
America - is the capital
of Paraná, the state of the
South. Everything works
like clockwork.
By contrast, this perfect
city has lost most of that
magic South American
atmosphere.

93 top Florianópolis is
the capital of the state of
Santa Catarina, in
southern Brazil. Founded
on an island, this
unusual city with a mild
climate and European
buildings boasts 42
beaches.

93 centre top Recife, the
capital of Pernambuco,
in the Brazilian
Northeast, is also known
as the Venice of Brazil for
its numerous bridges.
Recife is experiencing the
same problems as
Fortaleza: large-scale
tourism, social inequality
and a great deal of child
prostitution.

93 centre bottom
Fortaleza, the capital
of the state of Ceará,
Northeastern Brazil,
is the new tourist
destination of recent
years.

93 bottom The capital
of Rio Grande do Sul,
the southernmost state
of Brazil, Porto Alegre
is the home of gauchos,
the Brazilian cowboys.
The economy of the state
is based on cattle breeding
in large fazendas.

*94 top and bottom
The baroque interior
of the church of San
Francisco de Assís in
Salvador da Bahia
reaches a peak of
exaggeration. Every
inch of wall and
ceiling bears finely
worked inlays covered
with gold. Salvador,
like the mining town
of Ouro Preto, has
more churches than
houses, all built to show
the power of the
wealthy businessmen
and nobles. The places
of worship used by the
slaves are
distinguished by their
clean lines and simple
interiors.*

*94-95 The photo shows
the interior of São
Francisco de Assís
again. The best time
to admire the refined
inlays is during
services when the whole
nave is illuminated.*

95 top *The facade of São Francisco de Assis in Salvador da Bahia is shown in this photo. To the left of the church stands the Igreja da Ordem de Sao Francisco da Peniténcia, part of the same religious complex. The front is lined with statues and sculpted reliefs typical of Portuguese and Spanish baroque style.*

96-97 *The Capela Dourada in Recife stands opposite the law courts. It can be visited every day between 8.00 and 11.30 a.m. and between 2 and 5 p.m. Beside it is the Museu das Artes Sacras which has the same opening times.*

96 top left
The cathedral of
Nossa Senhora do
Pilar di São Joao del
Rei, Minas Gerais
was built in 1721 and
displays a wealth of
azulejos and gilded
altars.

96 top right
The Capela Dourada
in Recife belongs to
the third Order of São
Francisco and stands
in the Santo Antônio
district. Built in
1692, the project is
attributed to Antonio
Fernandes de Matos;
the reliefs showing the
Virtues are the work
of Antônio Santiago.

97 The church of
Nossa Senhora da
Conceiçao, Recife is
shown in these photos.

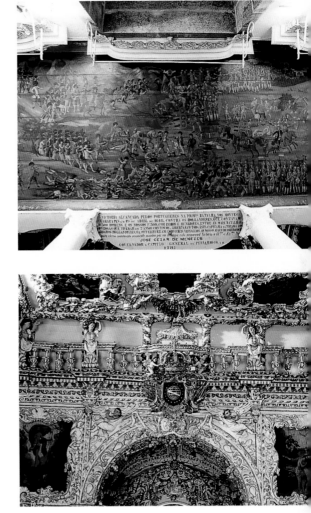

THE MANY ASPECTS OF BRAZIL

The mulatto has blue-green eyes, the Arab has slanting eyes, the African has blond hair and the European has the straight, black glossy hair typical of the Indian. If an experiment into mixing races had been specifically designed, it could not have succeeded better than in Brazil. It has taken 500 years to form *o povo brasileiro* (the Brazilian population), consisting of some 147 million inhabitants (according to the last census, taken in 1991, there will be 180 million by the year 2000) living in a huge territory of 8,511,965 square kilometres, over twice the size of India. Although Brazil has the fifth-largest population in the world, it is one of the least densely populated countries, with only 17 inhabitants per square kilometre. This distribution is obviously a mere average; in practice, most of the population is concentrated in the cities. According to a survey by IBGE (the Brazilian Institute of Statistical Geography), 75% of Brazilian families live in urban areas. In the State of Rio de Janeiro, for example, 90% of the inhabitants live in towns, while in the State of São Paolo, the proportion is 88%. Over half the population of Brazil, some 80 million people, is concentrated in the south-east of the country; this area, which might be described as the most industrialised and Europeanised part of Brazil, occupies only 10.85% of the country's territory. To continue with the statistics, over 40% of Brazilians are coloured; this means that Brazil now

has the largest mixed-race population in the world. So how was the Brazilian race formed? Many anthropologists agree that the first men to live in Latin American were people of Mongol origin who crossed the Bering Strait in the far north-east of the American continent after an ice age, probably pursuing animals fleeing from the freezing cold. This happened 15-25 thousand years before the arrival of Europeans on the continent. Some experts believe that the South American populations arrived not only from the Bering Strait but also from the south, from Polynesia and Australia, and that the Indians are a blend of the two races. Before the Portuguese arrived there were around 3 million Brazilian Indians, descendants of the first immigrants in human history.

98 and 99 Brazil is perhaps the only country on earth to contain all the races of the world - Indians, the original inhabitants; Africans, present in massive numbers in the states of Minas Gerais and Bahia, who arrived as slaves for the sugar and coffee plantations; Europeans (Germans, French, Dutch, Spanish, Russians and Italians); Arabs, Persians, Japanese and Chinese. Despite the apparent calm between different races Brazil has a classist society. Racism may not be clearly visible but it exists and is more a conflict of social standing than of skin colour.

After five hundred years of colonisation, compulsory and voluntary immigration and dominations which have united Africans and Amerindians, Europeans and Arabs, Japanese and Chinese, Asian Indians and Caucasians, the indigenous population has been reduced to some 270,000, and even that figure may well be an overestimate. The history of the Amerindians is one of massacres, violence and tyranny, and the Africans did not fare much better. Between

1531 and 1855 (when the slave trade was abolished), some 4 million Africans were deported to the new Portuguese colony. The numbers imported were so huge that in some parts of the country, such as Bahia, Pernambuco, Rio de Janeiro, Minas Gerais and Maranhão, the slave population outnumbered the free population. The colony's labour force came from the Gulf of Guinea, Angola and Mozambique. Many African men came from Islamicised areas, with the result that both their culture and their language were Arabic. Every African who arrived as a slave brought his own culture and preserved it jealously, handing it down it from generation to generation. That's why there is such a strong African influence in Brazilian culture, from music to animist cults and ritual festivals. In addition to African slaves there were also Oriental immigrants – Chinese, Koreans and above all, Japanese. The Japanese began to emigrate to the tropics in 1908. Organised in cooperatives, they specialised in producing and marketing fruit and vegetables and growing rice and tea. The largest number of immigrants came from Italy (especially the Veneto and Calabria regions), and mainly colonised the southern parts of the country.
In the State of Santa Catarina, for example, seven radio stations broadcast in Veneto dialect, the language spoken in many towns of southern Brazil.

100 top There is enormous black influence in the Brazilian culture: religious rites, animists, music and dancing. The samba, the most famous Brazilian dance, comes from the African savannah. The cultural hotbed of music and dancing is Bahia, where 90% of the population is black or mulatto.

100 bottom Gilberto Gil is one of Brazil's most famous musicians. Persecuted under the dictatorship as were other artists of the times, in the early Seventies he and Caetano Veloso invented tropicalism, an artistic and cultural movement that has influenced Latin-American music for the last thirty years.

100-101 The body-beautiful cult is very strong in Brazil. Jewellery, natural creams and fitness are manias that go beyond the bounds of the mere fad.

101 top Candomblé, *like voodoo a cult of Yoruba derivation, is the most widely-followed religion in Salvador da Bahia. Only followers can watch the ceremonies although often, for tourists and to earn some money, public rites are performed, but they are not carried through to the end.*

102 top right Cachoeira, a small, perfectly preserved colonial town in the state of Bahia, celebrates the Festa da Nossa Senhora de Boa Morte in the first fortnight in August. The event is 200 years old and commemorates the liberation of African women from slavery. Today it follows strict rituals, such as the request for donations, masses, processions, dinners and samba de roda.

102 bottom right Forty-five days after Easter Pirénópolis, a colonial city 60 miles or so from Goiânia, capital of the state of Goiás, is the scene of the Mediaeval Festa do Divino Espírito Santo. For three days it is the scene of tournaments, dances and religious rites that culminate in the battle between Moors and Christians. The Moors are defeated and converted to Christianity.

102 top left The congada is a celebration typical of the Northeast. It commemorates the coronation of a Congolese king which took place during slavery.

102 bottom left Another dance characteristic of the Northeast is Guerreiros. The dancers are dressed gaudily in multi-coloured costumes and hats shaped like churches, decorated with mirrors and trinkets.

The minority European colonies such as Poles and Slavs have actually inherited the Veneto dialect as their second language after Portuguese. It is consequently difficult to identify the Brazilians. Although some mysterious force has blended cultures and races, the genetic miracle has not eliminated racial rivalry. Racism, especially towards blacks and Indians, did not die out with the abolition of slavery in the nineteenth century. This is demonstrated by the fact that the poor who live

in conditions of penury in the *favelas* (shanty towns) are mainly blacks and north-easterners, close relations of the Indians. In Rio de Janeiro, for example, one inhabitant in three lives in the *favelas*, while in Belo Horizonte, capital of the State of Minas Gerais, the proportion is one in four. These poor living conditions are also reflected in the field of education: over 17 million people (more than 18% of the population aged over 14) are illiterate, and the figure is expected to rise to 23 million by the year 2000. The challenge of constructing a fairer Brazil has been taken up by the President, sociologist Fernando Henrique Cardoso, who has included education among the priorities in his government's manifesto. Has the time finally come when the gap between rich and poor, prosperous and destitute will be narrowed? Not many people think so, because Brazil also means destiny, living from day to day; in a nutshell, "*seja o que Deus quiser*" (may God's will be done).

103 The Lavagem do Bonfim is a traditional celebration held every year in January: the women dressed in characteristic white garments, wash the steps of the church of Nosso Senhor Bom Jesus do Bonfim; then comes a great popular festival. The sanctuary draws pilgrims from all over Brazil. Numerous miracles have occurred here and the sacristy contains a remarkable collection of ex-votos - plastic replicas of parts of the human body, crutches, plaster casts and even bullets.

104-105 Jangadas *at anchor on a Ceará beach. Fishing is one of the main activities in this state which includes the Sertao, the famous desert immortalized by Guimarães Rosa.*

104 top Fishermen on their jangadas, *rafts with a small sail, return to Canoa Quebrada. This beach, in the state of Ceará, became a gathering place for hippies in the Seventies.*

105 top Natal, the capital of the Rio Grande do Norte is famous for its as yet uncontaminated beaches dotted with fishing villages and for the enormous sand dunes that constantly change shape with the wind.

Fatalism, destiny, exaggerated optimism, delight in rhythm and colour and shameless nationalism are the characteristics of all Brazilians, whether they are black or yellow, white or half-caste. The samba, carnival and football (introduced in 1895 by an Englishman, Charles Miller) put this concept of life into practice. The samba originated with the tom-toms of Angola, while the carnival, introduced to Rio at the beginning of the colonial age, came from the Azores. Nowadays the samba schools parade in a street designed specially for the purpose by Oscár Niemeyer, called the "sambadrome"; it is 600 metres long, with terraces on either side that can hold 6,000 spectators. The entrance to this unusual monument to Brazilian joie de vivre is represented by two large convex concrete arches; not an abstract sculpture but the sensual, stylised representation of the curving buttocks of a mulatto girl, the Carnival Queen.

105 centre The photo shows a street child (menino de rua) in São Paulo. Abandoned children are one of Brazil's greatest problems. They start to sniff crack and carpenter's glue, robbing and stealing to survive and are persecuted by the death squads, often made up of off-duty policemen, who kill them without mercy.

105 bottom The characteristic traits of the people of the Northeast are a mixture of Indian, African and Dutch - those who landed here occupying the coasts of Pernambuco over the years.

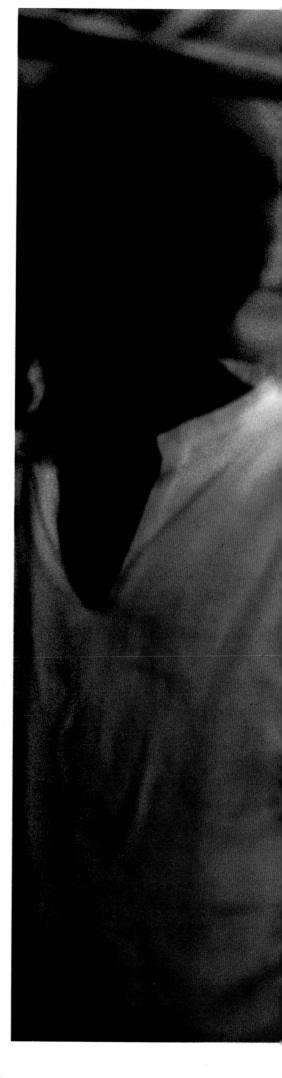

106 bottom left
The costumes of the filhas de santo, *the* candomblé *priestesses, are similar to those of the* Orixás, *the gods they impersonate. The girl in the picture represents* Oxúm, *the goddess of the rivers who corresponds to* Nossa Senhora de Aparecida.

106 top right
Spiritism and umbanda *are two more cults similar to* candomblé. umbanda *differs from* candomblé *in that communication with the spirits occurs through a medium and the* filhas de santo *are not usually directly possessed by the spirit.*

106 bottom right
A filha de santo *is shown in this photo. During ceremonies the priestesses incarnate the saint invoked by the gathering and to whom they are devoted. Possessed by the god they fall into a trance.*

106-107
A ceremony for the initiation of a candomblé *priestess, like many other cults, has a hierarchical structure and rites are celebrated in specific places, called* terreiros. *Candomblé initiation ceremonies are amply described by Jorge Amado, the most famous Brazilian writer.*

106 top left
A Bahian priestess of Iemanjá, *the queen of the sea and fish. In the religious syncretism that mixes Catholic saints with African divinities (a trick used by the* slaves to worship *their own gods) the goddess of the sea corresponds to* Nossa Senhora de Conceição *and is portrayed as a siren with a woman's torso and a fish tail.*

108-109
Carnival is certainly the most popular festival in Brazil. Although born in Bahia, it reigns supreme in Rio de Janeiro. In 1934 under the government of Getúlio Vargas the samba became the official dance of the Carnival and it is the symbol of this great festivity, imported from the Azores in the 17th century. Together with football it is one of the few moments that brings Brazilian society together: for this week all, rich and poor, meet up for the "pular carnaval na rua", dancing the samba in the streets with no distinction of race or class although most of the samba schools that participate in the traditional parades are of humble origin.

THE AMAZON, A LAND UNDER SIEGE

110-111 As well as the Amazon, the great river that crosses Brazil to flow into the Atlantic at Belém, there are countless other rivers (the largest tributaries of the Amazon include: the Negro, Içá, Yapurá and Trombetas rivers, to the left, and the Tapajós, Xingú, Javary, Jataí, Juruá, Tefé and Madeira rivers, to the right) as well as the igarapés that often form after the periodical forest floods.

110 top left As a result of high temperatures and heavy rains (94 inches per year) the Amazon soil has lost structure and nutrients becoming acid and not very fertile. Trees survive thanks to the humus produced by their own leaves.

110 top right Whenever the Amazon is mentioned the image conjured up is that of just a vast forest. Instead this huge area that fills more than half of Brazil (58.5%) contains an incredible variety of plants and animals.

Raoni, with the stately appearance of a chief, wearing glasses, a pair of threadbare jeans and a magnificent feathered headdress, his torso decorated and a wooden disc inserted in his bottom lip as a mark of rank, walks into the office of the Minister of the Interior in Brasilia carrying a TV camera. With him are a dozen members of the Kayapò tribe. They sit down on the large black leather sofas, cross their legs and wait, firmly holding onto their spears. They're going to talk to the minister about a delicate question; a TV crew from Rede Globo has entered their reserve and started filming without permission, and the Indians have confiscated the camera.

Now they're going to hand it over officially, on condition that the camera crew destroys the film. When the solemn act has been performed, the Indians leave as silently as they came. The man of government in his impeccable grey suit and the man of the forest, clad in little but his dignity, are worlds apart. This episode, recorded by the writer, took place a few years ago. Few Indians have survived in the great rain forest. There were three million of them in the Brazilian part of Amazonia before the Europeans arrived, but only 160,000 now, representing 60% of the 270,000 Amerindians living in Brazil. They include a few representatives from numerous tribes, as demonstrated by their speech. 150 different languages, divided into 12 linguistic families, are

spoken in Amazonia alone. 95,000 Indians live in the 216 areas officially registered and supervised by FUNAI (the National Indian Foundation), the government agency responsible for protecting them. These areas cover just over 55 million hectares, 10% of Amazonia. It's rather like relegating the former owners of a royal palace to the cellar. This huge green palace covers just over half the territory of Brazil, and is divided between nine States (Amazonas, Pará, Acre, Maranhão, Mato Grosso, Tocantins, Amapá, Rondônia and Roraima). It's 3,400 kilometres long from east to west and 2,000 kilometres from north to south, contains 30,000 classified species of plants and 15,000 species of animals, and only 10% of the population.

It would be quite wrong to consider the Amazonian Indian as the "noble savage". Many tribes are now Westernised, at least in terms of labour organisation. Some work as *seringeiros* (rubber tappers), others trade in wood, and others have set up well-equipped agricultural cooperatives. Few still live according to the ancient customs. Apart from the Indians there are also *caboclos*, of mixed Amerindian and white blood, and *cafusos*, of Amerindian and black African descent. They have lived in the forest for centuries, exploiting its natural resources such as rubber. Amazonia is often wrongly believed to be no more than a large uninhabited forest, all alike; a forest with no owners, which anyone can occupy and exploit. That must have been the attitude of the new colonists – foreign multinationals, large landowners, gold prospectors and adventurers of all kinds. The delicate Amazonian ecosystem is continually threatened by these random variables. The gold rush, which began as long ago as the sixteenth century, has now reached intolerable levels. Then, explorers were attracted by the legendary Kingdom of Manoa and its King (called El Dorado by the Spanish), who covered his naked body with gold dust every day. In 1540, Spanish explorer Francisco de Orellana crossed the entire Amazon basin in search of the golden king. Accompanied by a handful of men he reached his journey's end, but found no trace of the gold or the king. He travelled through dangerous, hostile country, and was the first to see what he described as "the tribe of women alone", the legendary Amazons after whom the forest is named. Manoa was probably discovered two centuries later by Francisco Raposo, a Portuguese explorer who described its impressive walls and great palaces. The legendary city was never rediscovered. Perhaps swallowed up by vegetation, it is still dreamed of by present-day Orellanas.

Gold has been found, however, and like the Klondike of old, has attracted thousands of prospectors. The best-known location (though there are hundreds like it) is the Sierra Pelada, a mountain ridge where a gold seam was discovered in the early Eighties.

The mountain was riddled with holes within a few years. The tireless *garimpeiros* (gold prospectors), coarsened by fatigue and gold fever, climb up and down steep ladders carrying bags of earth on their backs to be cleaned and sieved.

Everyone must have seen Sebastião Salgado's eloquent photos at least once; the Sierra Pelada looks like Dante's Inferno, a mass of desperate men frenetically searching for a few nuggets of gold, like thousands of dirty, ragged ants, living for an illusion.

Apart from having a devastating effect on the Indians, who were killed by diseases unknown to them or exterminated by the prospectors' rifles, the arrival of the *garimpeiros* took an equally dramatic toll on the forest. The rivers now contain large amounts of the mercury used to filter the gold (and the pollution affects human beings who eat fish full of the liquid metal), new towns that have upset the delicate balance of Amazonia have sprung up from nowhere, and landing strips and roads have been built, although the forest continues to reclaim them as it fights to survive.

114 top left, 114 right, 115 left, 115 right All the Indian tribes, the Kayapó *in particular devote great attention to the body. Tattoos, piercing, shell necklaces - all and anything that will add beauty. Besides the plants used to make dyes for the body, the Indians have exceptional knowledge of herbal medicine. Many of the ingredients and dishes used by the Indians in their cooking (*manioc*,* moqueca*, a Bahian dish made with fish and palm oil;* paçoca*, meat cooked with manioc) are now commonly found in Brazilian cuisine.*

114 bottom left Raoni, the memorable chief of the Kayapó*, wearing the traditional yellow head-dress, sign of leadership, and a lip disc, is the most famous of the Indian chiefs; he travelled the world with the English singer Sting seeking consensus and aid to save the Amazon.*

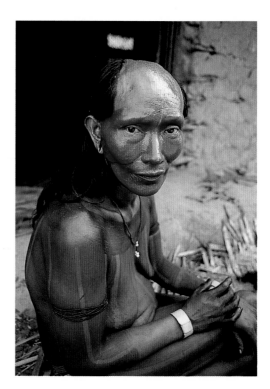

116-117
The Yanomami *Indians inhale a hallucinogenic powder called* yakoana *through a bamboo shoot to combat disease and enter in contact with the* hekurá, *the eternal spirits of nature. This drug is extracted from the seeds of a plant in August and September and the rite involves a ceremony with only male participation.*

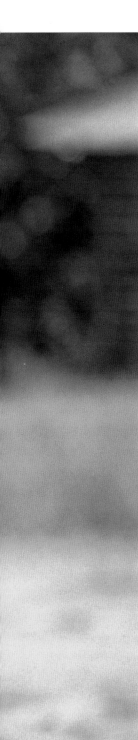

116 top left The Barbudos *Indians, a tribe recently discovered and apparently of Arara blood, are noted for their beards, an exception among the Indians who are normally smooth-skinned.*

116 top right The Poturú *Indians, the tribe that lives on the banks of the Rio Cupinapanema, northern Amazon, also have the custom of piercing their lips to insert large objects, both for beauty and as a sign of leadership.*

117 top The maloca *or aldeia is the large hut where the Indians live. Circular in form and open at the top, it houses numerous families.*

117 bottom The Yanomami *live in the state of Roraima and part of the Venezuelan Amazon. They have become known internationally for the battles fought against the large property owners and the garimpeiros who ten years ago invaded their territory with government consent (one of the sites for the mining of the precious metal had been established there).*

The natural devastation is accompanied by moral devastation. It is not unusual for Indian girls little more than 12 years old to be kidnapped and taken to these new towns (if a huddle of tumbledown shacks can be described as a town) to satisfy the appetites of the rough *garimpeiros.*

Other dangers also threaten the earth's last source of oxygen. The government's campaign to populate the Amazonas region has brought in a throng of poverty-stricken settlers and rich landowners, all attracted by the rock-bottom prices of the land (2,5 hectares – about 6 acres – costs the same as two cows) and the hope of a better life.

Hundreds of square kilometres of forest are systematically burnt to create pastures, in the belief that there will be enough grass to feed the herds. This is a pointless task, because the soil of Amazonia is poor, and the trees obtain their nourishment from the humus they themselves produce.

If the fertile part of the soil is destroyed, nothing else will grow. Fires leave the soil unprotected, leading to erosion; they reduce fertility and cause floods and the formation of new islands which prevent underwater life and hamper navigation through the hundreds of rivers and streams that wind through the rain forest.

The list of invaders of the forest is even longer: aluminium factories

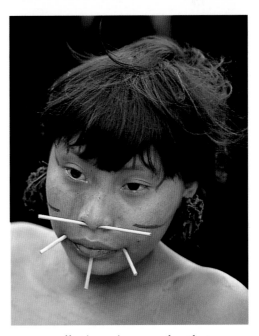

cause pollution, ironworks that use wood charcoal obtained from the trees to fuel their furnaces contribute to deforestation, and great hydroelectric plants flood acres of forest without regard for the people or animals living in them.

The picture is an unedifying one. However, something is changing in the green planet. Since the involvement of Chico Mendes (the rubber tappers' leader who was shot dead by cattle raiser Darli Albes), Sting,

Raoni, the Rio Conference (a major declaration of intent, but nothing more) and Marina Silva (a senator from Acre State who is the latest champion of the rain forest), deforestation has declined. According to the official figures it fell from 2.5 million hectares in 1988 to 900,000 in 1991 – a promising trend.

Everyone, all over the world, should care about the life of the great forest, because Amazonia does not only belong to the Brazilians, but to the whole planet; the life of the earth depends on Amazonia, and the life of Amazonia depends on the earth. Action must be taken before it's too late; the State of Rondônia has already lost 20% of its trees. The ideal solution would be to exploit the huge resources of the forest without destroying it. Apart from rubber and an immense amount of tropical fruit, the forest is also a huge pharmacy; 400 drugs have been developed from its plants so far. A utopian idea? Perhaps, but look at what happened during the rubber boom at the turn of the century. Brazil sold 88% of all the rubber exported in the world. That is how Manaus, the great palace in the middle of nowhere, came to be built.

The symbol of Manaus's wealth is the Opera House, built in 1896, which cost 10 million dollars at present values. The whole iron structure was assembled in Glasgow, the 66,000 coloured bricks that decorate the dome were imported from France, and the frescoes were commissioned from Italian painter Domenico de Angelis. The port on the River Amazon became one of the richest in the world. The splendour of Manaus came to an end shortly before the Great War, destroyed by the Asian plantations controlled by the British, who sold their rubber at a lower price. Those days are long past, swept away by relentless

progress and a great, slowly flowing river that discharges water into the Atlantic at the rate of 176,000 cubic metres a second. "The River Amazon", said famous author Mário de Andrade during a trip down the river in 1927, "is the final proof that monotony is one of the most magnificent elements of the sublime." How right he was. The landscape of the River Amazon and its 1,100 tributaries consists of mile after mile of trees. The river is navigable from Belém (in the State of Pará), where it flows into the Atlantic, to Iquitos in Peru, 3,700 kilometres away. The river is the natural highway of Amazonia, far more than the Trans-Amazonian Highway. The explorer's dream, the source of life for thousands of species of plants and animals, including man, and a fount of legends, the Amazon stands guard over its queen, the forest. Goodness knows how long the great Amazon artery will be able to go on pumping clean life-blood to provide its ancient owner with oxygen. A spark of life suddenly leaps out of the water and dives in again with a splash. It's a boto, a dolphin with a long nose that looks like a beak. In the culture of *umbanda*, the *candomblé* of the forest, the external genitals of the male and female boto are preserved. They are considered miraculous aids to love bonds and fertility – a symbol of love for the inhabitants of the forest and a symbol of hope for the tiny, frenetic life forms crowded together in the shelter of the Great Mother.

120 top The sloth (Bradypus tridactylus) is jokingly called bicho preguiça, lazy animal, by the Brazilians for its exasperatingly slow movements. This apparently harmless creature has a deadly grip.

120 bottom The anta, the Portuguese name for the tapir, lives all over the Latin American continent and can grow to 3 feet in height, 6 feet in length and weigh 400 pounds. It feeds on a diet of fruit and leaves and lives close to rivers.

120-121 The numerous monkey species that live in the forest include the nocturnal monkey which is fond of cane-brakes and feeds on their leaves.

121 top Besides its plant life the Amazon is also rich in animals, such as this Cyclopes didactilus. *Mexico is the only country in the world to boast a higher number of mammal species than Brazil's 450.*

122 The Amazon forest holds countless records. It has been calculated that one square mile of rain forest contains more living vegetable species than all of Europe and more than 60,000 plant species have been classified in the Brazilian Amazon alone. 87 different types of plant have been found per 2.5 acres at Belém whereas the figure for Manaus is 179.

123/126 The Amazon is commonly known as "the lungs of the world". This is incorrect as the huge quantity of oxygen produced by the forest is precisely the amount needed to keep its plants and living creatures alive. If anything, the Amazon is a huge reservoir of carbon and the fires lit for forced deforestation produce carbon dioxide, increasing the danger of a greenhouse effect on the planet.

130-131 Large, coloured bracts enclose the small green flowers of the Heliconia wagneriana, one of the hundreds of plants growing in the Amazon forest.

Mosquitoes and other small insects reproduce inside these natural cavities and the birds (like this white-bearded hermit) come here to feed and consequently pollinate the heliconia.

130 top Flowers are a characteristic feature of the great forest thanks to the particular humid microclimate generated by the trees which act as a greenhouse.

128 top left
The tucanuçu *(Rhamphastus toco) of the toucan family, is the symbol of Brazil and lives in small colonies nesting in cavities in high tree trunks. Toucan is also the name of an Indian tribe and a tongue spoken in the northwest Amazon.*

128 bottom left Numerous animal species live in the Amazon, some not yet classified. The queen of the reptiles is the anaconda, sucuri *in Portuguese, a snake that grows to 33 feet in length. Greyish-green in colour with symmetrical patches and a yellow belly, it lives in the water and feeds on fish, birds, mammals and even crocodiles, which it squeezes slowly until all the bones are broken and then swallows.*

128 top right Botos are frequently spotted when sailing along the Rio Amazonas. They will appear suddenly and follow the boats for long stretches. Their genitals (male and female) are dried and sold at the market by the curanderos *as powerful love remedies.*

128 bottom right There are 18 known species of piranha in Brazil. These range from a minimum of 7 to a maximum of 17 inches in size and their incredibly sharp teeth make them a hazard for the riveirinhos, *the inhabitants of the river banks. Extremely voracious, they are attracted by blood.*

129 The onça pintada, *the jaguar, is one of the most feared mammals in the great forest. But not only in the forest; this great cat lives practically all over Brazil with the exception of Rio Grande do Sul and the coastal states of the Northeast.*

127 *The Brazilian stretch of the Amazon river is fully navigable. The longest river in the world (4,247 miles against the 4,145 miles of the Nile) is on average approximately 98 feet deep. In some parts, such as the Obidos Strait, this reaches 330 feet. The maximum width is 9 miles at the confluence with the Rio Tapajós. During the rainy season the level of the river rises from 33 to 50 feet.*

131 top left The jambeiro *is a member of the myrtle family* (Eugenia malaccensis), *originating from India; it has large, brightly-coloured oblong leaves, conspicuous flowers with numerous stamens and a tasty purplish-red fruit.*

131 bottom left It has been calculated that Brazil has 55 thousand flower-producing plant species, most being found in the Amazon.

130 top right Very rarely does the same plant species constitute more than 20% of the vegetable population per acre in the Amazon. This means that the variety is enormous and it becomes hard to classify them all. There are over 400 known types of medicinal plants alone.

130 centre right and bottom right Brazil is one of the tropical countries where orchids flourish most successfully. Many of these flowers and plants present in the huge Amazon basin are also found in Africa because millions of years ago the two continents were joined.

INDEX

MUSEUM AND ART COLLECTIONS

Ancient Arts Museums—Lisbon:
page 30 bottom.

Civica raccolta stampe A. Bertarelli
Castello Sforzesco - Milan:
page 29 centre left.

Kunshitorisches Museum - Vienna:
page 22 top.

Library of Ajuda—Lisbon: page 28.

Miramare Castle—Italy: page 40.

National History Museum—
Rio de Janeiro: pages 20-21, 36 top
left, 38 top left, 39 bottom left, 41
right.

National Library—Rio de Janeiro:
pages 33 top left and bottom, 38
centre right, 39 bottom right, 42
top left, 42 centre right.

National Library of France—Paris:
page 38 bottom right.

Marine Museum—Lisbon:
pages 22-23.

Pierpoint Morgan Library:
pages 21 top, 30 top.

Ufficio Storico della Marina - Paris:
pages 30-31.

136 Arara and parrots are both symbols of Brazil. These animals live mostly in the immense pluvial Amazon basin and in Mata Atlántica.

Map: Patrizia Derossi